Electronic Music and
MIDI
Projects

R A Penfold

PC Publishing

PC Publishing
4 Brook Street
Tonbridge
Kent TN9 2PJ
UK

First published 1994
© PC Publishing

ISBN 1 870775 24 4

British Library Cataloguing in Publication Data

Penfold RA
  Electronic Music and Midi Projects
  I. Title
  786.7

ISBN 1-870775-24-4

Printed and bound in Great Britain by Bell & Bain, Glasgow

Preface

H ome made equipment has been part of the electronic music scene for just about as long as there has been electronic music. In the early days there was often no alternative to using home constructed equipment since ready made alternatives were conspicuous by their absence. Also, the commercial electronic music gear that was available tended to be quite expensive. Today's ready-made electronic instruments are much more affordable, but in many cases it is still possible to produce home constructed units for significantly less than the cost of broadly comparable ready made alternatives. It is also still possible to build effects units etc. that have no true commercial counterparts.

Whether you wish to save money, boldly go where no musician has gone before, rekindle the pioneering spirit, or simply have fun building some electronic music gadgets, the designs featured in this book should suit your needs. The projects are all easy to build, and some are so simple that even complete beginners at electronic project construction can tackle them with ease. The basic mixer, MIDI tester, MIDI lead tester, metronome, electronic swell pedal, THRU box, and MIDI automatic switcher are all well suited to beginners. Stripboard layouts are provided for every project, together with a wiring diagram. The mechanical side of construction has largely been left to individual constructors to sort out, simply because the vast majority of project builders prefer to do their own thing in this respect.

None of the designs requires the use of any test equipment in order to get them set up properly. Where any setting up is required, the procedures are very straightforward, and they are described in detail.

The projects in this book are primarily aimed at keyboard players. Guitarists are catered for in a separate book *Electronic Projects For Guitar* from the same publisher and author as this publication.

Contents

Getting started | 1

The projects featured in this book should present few difficulties to anyone who has some previous experience of electronic project construction. In fact many of the projects are simple enough for complete beginners at electronics, but there is some essential background information that must be acquired before anyone new to this type of thing starts soldering in earnest. In this chapter it is not possible to provide a complete course on electronic components, methods of construction, etc. What is provided is an introduction to the components, construction techniques, etc. that are needed in order to build the particular projects described in this book.

With this information, a certain amount of skill, some common sense, and a bit of ingenuity, practically anyone should be able to build the more simple of the projects. If you are not a very practical sort of person, then I would be misleading you to say that you could still complete these projects successfully. It would not be true either, to say that an average beginner could successfully tackle the more complex of the projects featured in this book. However, provided you are not completely useless when it comes to manual skills, and you start with the simple projects first, it should not be too difficult to build these projects.

Components

The range of electronic components currently available to amateur users is vast. There are literally thousands of different components available. Fortunately, only a fairly small percentage of these are used in the projects featured here. This makes it relatively easy to obtain and identify the components. If you do not already have one of the larger electronic component mail order catalogues, then I would strongly advise getting at least one of these before starting to buy any of the components for a project.

If you are lucky enough to live near a branch of one the large electronic component retailers, then you may be able to obtain everything you need locally. Even if this should be the case, it is still worthwhile having one or two of the catalogues. These contain a mass of useful data, and also have lots of photographs or drawings of the compo-

Photo 1.1
A Resistor
B Radial electrolytic capacitor
C Ceramic capacitor
D Axial electrolytic capacitor
E Polyester capacitor
F Preset resistor

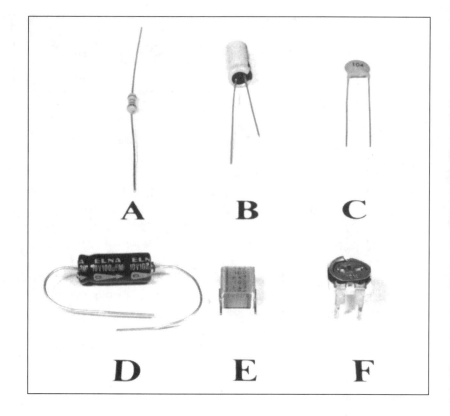

Photo 1.2
A Diode
B Transistor
C LED
D 8 pin DIL IC
E 14 pin DIL IC
F 16 pin DIL IC

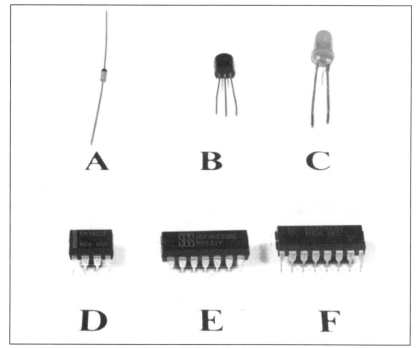

nents. These are very useful for beginners, as they make it relatively easy to find the right components. To put things another way, it reduces the risk of wasting time and money buying the wrong thing. If you do not live near to a suitable shop, then a catalogue and mail order buying represent the only practical method of obtaining the components you will need for these projects.

Resistors

Resistors must be the most common of electronic components. Practically every electronic project uses some of these, and in most cases they represent about half the components in a project. There are numerous different types of resistor available, but for most of the projects in this book ordinary carbon film resistors will suffice. You may find that some suppliers do not sell carbon film resistors. This is normally where they have rationalised their resistor stocks, and offer the higher quality metal film type as their 'bog standard' resistor.

The extra quality of metal film resistors is unlikely to bring any significant benefits with most of the projects featured here, but it will obviously not do any harm either. Metal film resistors are perfectly suitable for these projects, but where carbon film types are available they will do the job just as well but at a much lower cost.

Resistor values

The values of resistors are specified in ohms. The greek letter omega (Ω) is still used as an abbreviation for ohms, but these days a capital 'R' is more commonly used. Thus a 10 ohm resistor will often be referred to as a 10R component. In fact a value of 10R, particularly on circuit diagrams, is often just given as '10'. An ohm is a very small unit, and many of the resistors used in electronics have values of thousands of ohms, or even millions of ohms. One thousand ohms equal one kilohm, and the abbreviation 'k' is often used for kilohms. A million ohms is a megohm, or just 'M'.

A 33000 ohm resistor would therefore normally have its value given as 33 kilohms, or just 33k. A 1500000 ohm resistor has a value of 1.5 megohms, or just 1.5M for short. The letter which indicates the unit in use is often used to indicate the decimal point as well. Thus a 4R7 resistor is a 4.7 ohm type, a 5k6 resistor is a 5.6 kilohm (5600 ohm) component, and a 1M8 resistor is a 1.8 megohm (1800000 ohm) type. The point of this system is that it enables values to be represented using as few digits as possible. This is especially useful when trying to find space for the labels on circuit diagrams.

Resistors are available only in certain values, known as preferred values. This is what is generally known as the E24 series of values:

1.0	1.1	1.2	1.3	1.5	1.6
1.8	2.0	2.2	2.4	2.7	3.0
3.3	3.6	3.9	4.3	4.7	5.1
5.6	6.2	6.8	7.5	8.2	9.1

This series of values might look a little odd, but it operates on the principle of having each value about 10% higher than the previous one. This ensures that whatever the calculated value for a resistor might be, there will always be an actual resistor available that is within a few percent of this value. Note that components are not just available in these values, but also in their decades. In other words, as well as (say) 2.2 ohm resistors, there are also 22R, 220R, 2k2, 22k, 220k, and 2M2 types available. Resistors are not generally available with values higher than 10M, and so you will probably not find 22M types listed in components catalogues.

Resistor tolerances

Resistors have a tolerance rating, and this is usually 5% (possibly 10% on the higher values). The actual value of a resistor is never precisely its marked value. The tolerance rating is merely an indication of the maximum error. For example, a 100k 5% resistor would have an actual value of between 95k (100k minus 5%) and 105k (100k plus 5%). Ordinary 5/10% resistors are fine for the projects in this book. If your component supplier sells metal film resistors as their standard type, then these will have a tolerance of just 1% or 2%. These are a bit over-specified for our purposes, but are otherwise perfectly suitable for use in these projects.

Power ratings

Last, and by no means least, resistors have a power rating. This is basically just the maximum power in watts that the resistor can withstand. Practical power ratings tend to be a bit misleading as they are often quoted for different operating conditions. A 0.6 watt resistor might have a power rating that represents something close to the point where the component burns up, whereas a 0.25 watt type might have a rating that represents a very safe maximum dissipation figure. Their real power handling abilities might therefore be quite similar, despite the fact that the power ratings are very different. For these projects 0.25 watt resistors will suffice. Higher power types,

4

such as 0.33, 0.4, 0.5, and 0.6 watt types are also suitable, provided they are miniature types. Resistors such as old style 0.5 and 1 watt resistors are fine from the electronic point of view, but you are unlikely to be able to fit them into the component layouts provided here!

Colour coding

It is very unusual for resistors to have their values marked in numbers and letters. With high power types you do sometimes find that the value is written on as 4R7, 68R, or whatever, plus a letter to show the tolerance. It is many years since I last saw any small resistors which use this method though. The standard method of value marking is to have four coloured bands. This method of coding works in the manner shown in Figure 1.1, and Table 1. In theory, the first band is the one nearest to one end of the resistor's body. I would have to say that with all the small resistors in my spares box the two end bands are an equal distance from their respective ends of the body. However, it is still easy enough to tell which band is which, as the fourth band is well separated from the other three.

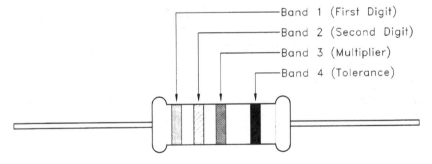

Band 1 (First Digit)
Band 2 (Second Digit)
Band 3 (Multiplier)
Band 4 (Tolerance)

Figure 1.1 The standard four band method of marking values onto resistors.

The first two bands indicate the first two digits of the value. For example, if these bands are respectively green and blue, the first two digits are 5 and 6, as can be seen from Table 1. The third band is the multiplier, and this basically just indicates the number of zeros that must be added to the first two digits in order to give the full value. For instance, if the third band is orange, this indicates that the first two digits must be multiplied by 1000, or that three zeros must be added in other words. Thus in our example value, we have 56 plus three zeros, or a value of 56000 ohms (56k). Band number four indicates the tolerance of the component. This will usually be gold, which indicates a tolerance of five percent.

This colour coding system can be a little confusing at first, but it has the advantage that the value markings are not easily obliterated. Even if the coloured bands should become chipped or worn, there will probably still be enough left to permit the value to be reliably deciphered. With tiny lettering on miniature resistors, it would be difficult to read the values even if the lettering was in perfect condition.

Table 1

Colour	Band	1/2	Band 3	Band 4
Black	0	x1	-	
Brown	1	x10	1%	
Red	2	x100	2%	
Orange	3	x1000	-	
Yellow	4	x10000	-	
Green	5	x100000	0.5%	
Blue	6	x1000000	0.25%	
Violet	7	-	0.1%	
Grey	8	-	-	
White	9	-	-	
Gold	-	-	5%	
Silver	-	-	10%	
None	-	-	20%	

There is a slight problem with resistor colour coding in that there are also a couple of five band codes in use. These are closely based on the standard four band type. With one of these five band codes you have what is basically the ordinary four band code, plus an extra band which indicates the temperature coefficient. The latter is a measure of how much the component's resistance changes with variations in temperature. This is something that is not normally of any interest, and the extra band can be ignored. There is an alternative (and rare) five band code which has the first three bands to indicate the first three digits of the value. The last two digits indicate the multiplier value and tolerance in the normal way. If a retailer is selling resistors with one of these five band codes, then their catalogue should give details of the code in use.

Potentiometers

A potentiometer is a form of resistor, but one where the value can be varied. A normal potentiometer has a control shaft which is fitted with a control knob. There is also a mounting nut and bush so that it can be fixed to the front panel of the case.

For the projects featured here it is the small carbon potentiometers that are required, not high power types such as wirewound potentiometers. Usually the mounting bush is for a 10 millimetre diameter hole, and the control shaft is 6 millimetres in diameter. However, some modern potentiometers have smaller mounting bushes and (or) shafts. Some, for instance, have the standard 6 millimetre shaft diameter, but require a mounting hole of just 7 millimetres in diameter. These miniature types are suitable for the projects featured here provided you remember to make the smaller mounting holes that they require. It is probably best to avoid types which have a control shaft diameter of other than 6 millimetres unless you are sure that you can obtain control knobs to fit them.

Preset potentiometers are physically very different from the standard variety. These are small components, and are often of open construction. Fortunately, it seems to be increasingly common for these components to have a plastic outer casing to keep dust and other contamination away from their inner workings.

For these projects it is the sub-miniature (0.1 or 0.15 watt) horizontal mounting type that is required. Other types are suitable electrically, but will probably not fit into the component layouts properly, and could be very expensive in the case of high quality multi-turn types.

Preset potentiometers are only generally available as linear types incidentally. Because of this, components lists do not normally specify whether a preset should be a logarithmic or a linear type, and component catalogues do not normally specify the type either. Unless stated otherwise, preset potentiometers can be assumed to be linear types.

Note that colour coding is not normally used for marking potentiometer values. Instead, the value is simply marked as '4k7 lin', or whatever. In some cases a letter 'A' after the value is used to denote a logarithmic component, or a letter 'B' is used to shown that it is a linear type. Colour coding is occasionally used for marking values on preset resistors. This coding is normally in the form of three coloured dots which indicate the value in the same way as the first three bands of a normal resistor colour code.

As far as their electrical characteristics are concerned, there are two types of potentiometer. These are the logarithmic ('log') and linear ('lin') types.

A linear potentiometer is the normal kind, where setting the control at a roughly mid-setting gives about half maximum resistance.

A logarithmic potentiometer has a very non-linear resistance characteristic. Adjustment towards one end of the track has little effect, while adjustment at the opposite end results in large changes in value. Logarithmic potentiometers are mainly used as volume controls, while linear potentiometers are used for practically all other potentiometer applications.

The components lists always specify which type is needed. Using the wrong type will not prevent a project from working, but you will get some strange control characteristics. This can make the projects difficult to use properly, so I would strongly recommend that the specified types should always be used.

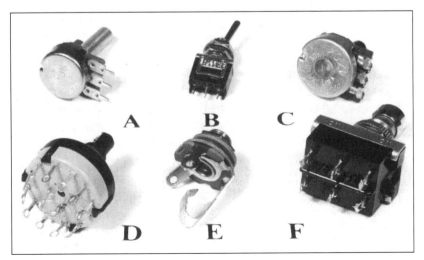

Photo 1.3
A Miniature potentiometer
B Miniature toggle switch
C Potentiometer
D Rotary switch
E Standard jack socket
F Heavy-duty push-button switch

Capacitors

Capacitors represent another type of component that is used in large numbers in electronic circuits. In a few projects they actually outnumber the resistors. The values of capacitors are in farads, but one farad is a massive amount of capacitance. Therefore, most 'real world' capacitors have their values marked in microfarads, nanofarads, or picofarads. Table 2 shows the relationship between these three units of measurement. A microfarad is one millionth of a farad incidentally. The abbreviations 'u', 'n', and 'p' are often used for microfarads, nanofarads, and picofarads respectively.

Table 2

Unit	Microfarads	Nanonfarads	Picofarads
Microfarads	1	1000	1000000
Nanofarads	0.001	1	1000
Picofarads	0.000001	0.001	1

Capacitor types

There are numerous different types of capacitor available. Here we will consider only the types that are relevant to the projects in this book. Where low values are called for, by which I mean values of under one nanofarad, ceramic plate capacitors are suitable. These are very small, square, plate-like components with the two leadout wires coming from one edge of the component. The values are usually marked in picofarads on the very low values (e.g. 27p = 27 picofarads). Values of more than 100 picofarads are sometimes marked in a slightly cryptic fashion, with the value being given in nanofarads. Thus 'n10' is 0.10 nanofarads or 100 picofarads, and 'n39' is 0.39 nanofarads or 390 picofarads. This is basically the usual method of using the units indicator to also show the position of the decimal point, but no leading zero is included.

There can be a problem with ceramic plate capacitors in that some of the components currently being sold have very short leadout wires indeed. In some cases these will fit into the component layouts without any difficulty, but in a few cases it might be necessary to solder short extension wires to their leadout wires in order to fit them into the component layouts properly.

Polystyrene components are also suitable where values of under one nanofarad are called for. The only proviso here is that they must be physically small types. There should be no problem if modern components are used, and you do not order a type intended for operation at very high voltages. The values of small polystyrene capacitors are normally marked on the components in picofarads, possibly with the tolerance shown as well, or a code letter to show the tolerance. Ordinary 5% tolerance polystyrene capacitors are suitable for these projects.

For values from one nanofarad to around one microfarad the component layouts are designed to take printed circuit mounting polyester capacitors. These have very short leadout wires that are really more like pins than normal leadout wires. This means that the component layouts have to be designed to suit components of a particular lead spacing. In this case a lead spacing of 7.5 millimetres (0.3 inches) is used for virtually all the medium value capacitors. Check the component layouts and be careful to order components that have the appropriate lead spacing.

It is only fair to warn you that the likely result of trying to manipulate polyester capacitors which have the wrong lead spacing into these component layouts is that leadout wires will become detached from the capacitors. In days gone by these polyester capacitors were very easily damaged in this way. Modern types seem to be much tougher, but they are still likely to be damaged if you bend the wires to suit a different lead spacing.

Capacitor markings

The values of polyester capacitors are normally marked on the components in nanofarads or picofarads, as appropriate. A 2.2 nanofarad component would therefore be marked '2n2', a 10n component would be marked '10n', and a 470nf (0.47uf) component would be marked 'u47'.

In a few cases ceramic capacitors are specified for values of around 100 nanofarads. These higher value ceramic capacitors have very inaccurate values, but they work well at high frequencies. This makes them well suited to certain applications, including decoupling types. It does not matter which type of ceramic capacitor is used, but disc types are the most widely available, and are generally the cheapest. Obviously you should avoid very high voltage types, or any special ceramic types which are expensive or physically quite large.

The value of ceramic capacitors is often just marked in nano or microfarads. Probably the most common method of value marking though, is one which uses three numbers. The first two numbers are the first two digits of the value. The third number is the number of zeros that must be added to these in order to give the value in picofarads. For a 100 nanofarad capacitor the marking would be '104'. The first two digits of the value are '1' and '0', and four zeros must be added to these. This gives a value of 100000 picofarads, which is the same as 100 nanofarads.

Electrolytics

Ordinary capacitors are not a very practical proposition where high values of more than about one microfarad are required. They are expensive to produce, and tend to be physically quite large. For high values it is normal to use electrolytic capacitors. These are not without their drawbacks, such as relatively high tolerances and high leakage currents, but they are adequate for many purposes where high values are needed.

The most important difference between electrolytic and non-electrolytic capacitors is that the electrolytic types are polarised. In other words they have positive and negative terminals, and must be connected into circuit the right way round if they are to function properly. Ordinary capacitors such as polyester and ceramic types, and resistors, can be fitted either way round.

Identification

Identifying the positive and negative leadout wires should not be difficult, since there are usually '+' and '-' signs marked on the body of an electrolytic capacitor which clearly show which lead is which. There seems to be a tendency these days towards marking only one lead or the other, but this is obviously all you need in order to get the component fitted round the right way.

Physically there are two different types of electrolytic capacitor. These are the radial and axial types. These are actually general terms which are applied to other types of component, but which are mainly encountered when dealing with electrolytic capacitors. An axial type is the usual tubular bodied component having a leadout wire protruding from each end. These would normally be mounted horizontally on the circuit board. A radial component has both leadout wires coming from the same end of the component, and it is intended for vertical mounting. It is usually possible to fit a radial capacitor into a layout that is designed for an axial type, or vice versa. Some careful forming of the leadout wires may be needed, or some extension wires might have to be added to the leadout wires.

It is best to avoid this type of thing though. Apart from the fact that it will give some slightly scrappy looking results, it is likely to result in components being something less than firmly fixed in place. This leaves the board vulnerable to problems with broken leads or short circuits from component lead to another. Incidentally, you will notice that axial electrolytics have an indentation around one end of the component's body. This is used to indicate the end of the component from which the positive (+) lead emanates. The '+' and (or) '-' markings are usually included as well, but the indentation enables you to see the polarity at a glance, making these markings largely superfluous.

Incidentally, radial capacitors are also known as PC (printed circuit) capacitors. This is actually a term which can be applied to any component which is intended for vertical mounting on a printed circuit board. In the early days of electronics all two-lead components were of the axial type. When printed circuits came along, these vertically mounting components were designed specifically to give compact component layouts with the new method of construction. Hence these became known as printed circuit mounting components, and eventually just PC components.

Voltage rating

With non-electrolytic capacitors you do not normally need to worry about the maximum voltages they can safely handle. The voltage ratings are generally around the 100 volt mark, or in some cases even higher. The projects in this book mostly operate on a 9 volt battery supply.

The situation is slightly different with electrolytic capacitors. The smaller values generally have voltage ratings of about 50 volts or more, but the higher values can have voltage ratings as low as 6 volts, or possibly even 3 volts. The components lists therefore give voltage ratings for electrolytics that are the minimum requirements. Any voltage ratings equal to or higher than these are suitable, provided the components are physically small enough to fit into the available space. If a 1u 10V component is specified, there should be no difficulty in using a 1u 100V type, which (if it is a modern component) should be physically quite small. On the other hand, you are unlikely to get away with using a 220u 100V component where a 220u 10V type is specified. A capacitor having such a high value and operating voltage would almost certainly be quite large.

The metronome project requires a capacitor that can be either a high quality electrolytic type, or a tantalum bead capacitor. From the user's point of view there is little difference between a tantalum capacitor and a radial electrolytic type. The tantalum capacitors are literally bead-like in appearance, and they are probably the best choice where a high quality, high value capacitor is needed.

Note that with the lower values of around 1u to 10u, most component suppliers no longer list components having low operating voltages. There is then no option but to opt for components having operating voltages of around 50 to 100 volts. These should be physically small components though, and they should fit into these component layouts with no difficulty.

Diodes

A diode is a type of semiconductor (like transistors and integrated circuits), but is the most simple type of semiconductor. It acts like a sort of electronic valve which enables an electric current to flow in one direction, but not the other. These components are also called rectifiers. The only difference between a rectifier and a diode is that the former is used in medium and high power applications, whereas a diode is used for small signals. Only diodes are used in the projects featured in this book.

Obviously a diode or rectifier must be connected the right way round if it is to let the current flow in the right direction. The standard method of polarity marking for diodes and the smaller rectifiers is to have a band marked around one end of the component's body. This indicates the cathode (+) leadout wire. The component layout diagrams in this book show this band on the diodes, so all you have to do is fit these components onto the board so that they match up with the diagrams in this respect. You do not really need to worry about what the terminals are called.

Diodes, like all semiconductors, do not have values. Instead they have type numbers, and the data sheet for each component shows its electrical ratings and characteristics. To make it easier to find the particular semiconductor you require, most component catalogues list diodes, rectifiers, transistors, etc. separately. The diodes used in these projects are all very common types which you should be able to find listed in any electronic components catalogue.

Soldering semiconductors

It is worth mentioning here that semiconductors are rather more vulnerable to heat damage than are most other electronic components. Modern silicon devices are somewhat more hardy in this respect than the old germanium based devices. However, even the silicon based devices need to be treated with due respect when they are being soldered into circuit. You can buy an implement called a heat-shunt. This clips onto leadout wires, and removes much of the heat that flows up the wires towards the bodies of components when soldered joints are being produced. I have never found it necessary to use one of these, but I do make sure that every soldered joint is completed fairly rapidly. If it becomes evident that a joint is not proceeding well, it is better to abandon it and try again once everything has cooled down, rather than pressing on and possibly damaging the component.

It is worth bearing in mind that no electronic components are totally heat-proof. Even with simple components such as resistors you can cause damage if you keep the bit of the soldering iron in place for so long that the component becomes discoloured and smoke begins to rise! Components will often survive this sort of treatment, but often with shifted values or other problems that will degrade performance. Try to complete all soldered joints reasonably quickly, preferably taking no more than a second or two.

LEDs

Several projects utilize light emitting diodes (LEDs). These are true diodes, but are used as indicator lights rather than because a diode action is required. The fact that they will only conduct in one direction is still of practical importance though. Unlike a filament bulb, a LED must be connected the right way round or it will not light up. In the past, most LEDs had a 'flat' on their body next to the cathode (+) leadout wire. This is less common than it once was, but it is still a feature of many LEDs. The other common method of showing LED polarity is to have the cathode leadout slightly shorter than the anode one. This method now seems to be the standard one, and all the LEDs I have obtained in recent years have had a shorter cathode lead. If in doubt you can always use trial and error. Connecting a LED the wrong way round is unlikely to cause any damage. The LED will simply fail to light up.

Transistors

The components discussed so far have all been two lead types. Transistors have three leadout wires, or in a few cases four leads. The circuits featured here only use the normal three leadout variety. The terminals of a transistor are called the base, emitter, and collector (often just abbreviated to b, e, and c respectively). The component layout diagrams featured in this book do not necessarily include identification letters for the leadout wires of transistors. This is simply because in most cases it is obvious how the component should be fitted onto the board if you look at the diagram and the component itself. Simply fit the components with the orientation shown in the diagrams, avoiding any crossed-over leadout wires. Note that where a leadout diagram for a transistor is shown, it is the convention that a base view is shown (i.e. the component is shown looking onto the leadout wires).

In many component catalogues there are dozens or even hundreds of different transistors listed. The transistors used in the projects featured here are all very common types. These should be listed in any electronics component catalogue, and should be amongst the cheapest of the transistors in the catalogue. Transistors are normally listed in the catalogues in some sort of alpha-numeric order, so it should not be too difficult to locate the right type numbers.

Integrated circuits

Modern electronic circuits tend to be extremely complex – even the simple ones. This might seem to be an impossible state of affairs, but it is made possible by integrated circuits (i.c.s). Strictly speaking each i.c. is a single component. However, it actually contains the equivalent of what could be anything from two to over one million components. Although a project might only use a dozen components, two of these could be i.c.s, each containing the equivalent of hundreds or thousands of components. This brings tremendous benefits to the electronics hobbyist. Many projects that would otherwise be impracticable are brought within the scope of many constructors. Integrated circuits can be used to reduce component counts to a realistic level, and also help to keep down costs. Very simple projects that actually do something useful become a practical proposition.

Some i.c.s are quite cheap, and cost pence rather than pounds. Where possible, the projects in this book are based on low cost devices that are available from practically every component supplier. In a few cases there is no choice but to opt for specialist devices that are less widely available and more expensive. Where a device is not widely available, the components list will mention one or two sources.

There are many hundreds of i.c.s listed in most components catalogues. In order to make it easier to find the devices you require it is standard practice for the integrated circuits to be listed in several categories. Most of the devices used in these projects are 'linear' integrated circuits. The only non-linear types used in these projects are 4000 series CMOS, the 6402 UART and the 74 series TTL logic devices. Any component catalogue should have a CMOS logic section which lists the appropriate devices. There should also be lists of the various TTL logic families (standard 74, 74HC, 74LS, etc.). As there are many instances of totally different integrated circuits with very similar type numbers, you need to be careful when ordering these components. The 6402 UART will be listed as a computer peripheral.

Type numbers

Another point to bear in mind is that the same device might be produced by two or more manufacturers, but under slightly different type numbers. There is a popular linear device called the uA741C. This was the type number used by the original manufacturer, and it is still specified as such in many components lists, including some of those in this book. However, it is now produced under type numbers such as LM741C, MC741C, and CA741C.

In components catalogues a device such as this might be listed under one specific type number, or even two or three different type numbers if the retailer stocks components from more than one source. In many cases though, popular integrated circuits which are produced by several manufacturers are simply listed under a sort of generic type number, which in this example would just be '741' or '741C'. Where necessary, the text for a project will include advice which should help you to find the right component.

I.C.s come in a variety of shapes and sizes. Many devices are available in more than one encapsulation. However, in component catalogues you will normally only find the DIL (dual in-line) versions listed. These are basically rectangles of black plastic which contain the silicon chip, with a row of metal pins along each long edge of the plastic case. It is from these two lines of pins that the DIL name is derived. Most integrated circuits have 8, 14, or 16 pins, but they can have anything from four to 40 or more pins. The projects featured here only have 8, 12, 14, or 16 pins though.

Static electricity

Some i.c.s are built using some form of MOS (metal oxide silicon) technology, and the practical importance of this is that they are sensitive to static voltages. A large static charge could probably damage any integrated circuit, but charges of this magnitude are not to be found in normal environments. MOS components can be damaged by relatively small static charges, such as those that tend to be generated by nylon carpets, clothes made from synthetic fabrics, etc. The risk of components being damaged in this way has perhaps tended to be exaggerated slightly. Manufacturers warnings can give the impression that MOS devices will be instantly destroyed unless they are stored and handled under carefully controlled conditions using thousands of pounds worth of specialised equipment!

In reality the risk is normally quite small. Many electronics hobbyists do not bother with any special handling precautions at all when dealing with MOS components, and in the main get away with it. However, when dealing with the more expensive MOS components it would seem to be prudent to exercise reasonable care. In fact it is not a bad idea to take a few simple precautions even when dealing with the cheaper components.

The most important of these is to leave static-sensitive components in their anti-static packaging until it is time to fit them onto the circuit board. Any MOS device should be supplied in some form of anti-static packing. This is usually conductive foam, ordinary plastic foam with a metal foil covering, a plastic tube, or a blister pack with a metal covering on the backing card. The basic idea is to either insulate the component from static charges, or (more usually) to short circuit all the pins together. This second method does not keep static charges away from the components, but it does ensure that dangerous voltages can not exist from one pin to another. It is a large voltage difference across the pins of a device that can actually cause damage.

Another important precaution is to avoid soldering MOS integrated circuits direct to the component panel. It is much safer if a suitable DIL integrated circuit holder is soldered to the board, and the MOS Integrated circuit is then plugged into the holder. It is best to leave out the integrated circuits until a project has been completed in all other respects.

The other main anti-static precaution is to simply avoid getting the devices in contact with any likely sources of high static voltages. For example, when constructing projects avoid wearing clothing made with synthetic fibres. When fitting MOS devices into their holders, try to avoid touching the pins as far as possible. In practice it might be impossible to avoid this completely. You often have to pinch the two rows of pins inwards slightly in order to get the integrated circuits into their holders. It is essential that integrated circuits are fitted the right way round. Get one of these components the wrong way round, and it could easily be destroyed when the project is switched on. Unfortunately, it is probably true to say that, in general, the more expensive the integrated circuit, the more vulnerable it is to damage from this sort of treatment.

To make it easy to get integrated circuits the right way round they have an indentation next to pin 1, plus a 'U' shaped notch at this end of the component. Figure 1.2 shows the notch and the 'dimple', and as is the convention, the integrated circuit is shown viewed from above. Note that this is the opposite to transistors, which are normally shown as base views in leadout diagrams. It is a 14 pin DIL device that is shown in Figure 1.2, but the same method is used for all normal DIL integrated circuits.

When building projects you do not normally need to worry about the pin numbering. Just get the devices orientated so that the notches and 'dimples' match up with the markings in the component layout diagrams. It is only fair to point out that many integrated circuits seem to have just the notch or only the 'dimple', but not both. This

I would strongly urge the use of holders for all integrated circuits, regardless of whether or not they are MOS devices. If you should accidentally fit an integrated circuit the wrong way round, there is little difficulty in gently prising it free from the holder using a small screwdriver, and then fitting it the right way round. Desoldering a multi-pin component from a circuit board can be quite difficult even if you do have access to proper desoldering equipment. Presumably many of the people tackling these projects will not have access to anything more than some very basic desoldering gear.

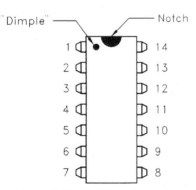

Figure 1.2 DIL pin numbering

does not really matter, since either one of them will enable you to get the device orientated correctly. Slightly confusingly, some devices have a sort of notch at the opposite end of the case to the proper one. This is presumably just some sort of moulding mark, and it is not usually difficult to see which is the proper notch and which is not.

The rest
Plugs and sockets

Only two types of socket are used in these projects. The audio inputs and outputs all use standard 0.25 inch (6.35 millimetre) jack sockets. This is probably the most common type of socket in electronic music systems, but it is obviously quite in order to use a different type of connector if it will fit in better with your particular setup. However, if you use a different type, make quite sure that you get it wired-up the right way round. Ordinary open type sockets are shown in the wiring diagrams, and these are the cheapest type.

There are also insulated sockets, which are an enclosed type having a plastic casing. They invariably seem to have some switch contacts that are activated by inserting and removing the jack plug. These contacts are of no use in the current context and simply confuse matters. Any mono jack sockets are usable, but unless you know what you are doing I would recommend the use of the open type, chassis mounting sockets, which have no switch contacts. These require 9.5 millimetre diameter mounting holes incidentally.

The other type of socket used in these projects is the 5 way DIN type used for MIDI inputs and outputs. There are numerous different types of DIN socket available, including at least three different 5 way types. The MIDI projects featured here require the 5 way 180 degree type. These have the five tags arranged in a 180 degree arc, and are also known as 5 way DIN sockets 'type A'. It is chassis mounting sockets that are needed, not printed circuit mounting types. These require a main mounting hole about 14 millimetres in diameter. Two 3.3 millimetre diameter holes are required for the metric M3 or 6BA mounting bolts. Once the main cutout has been made, the socket itself can be used as a sort of template to help mark the positions of the two smaller holes.

Switches

Most of the projects use one or more switches, and these are mostly very simple switches. In the components lists I have mainly specified sub-miniature toggle switches. A toggle switch is simply one that is controlled via a small lever (known as a 'dolly'). The sub-miniature versions of these switches are extremely small, reasonably cheap, and seem to be quite reliable these days. However, other types of switch, such as slider, rocker, and rotary types are also suitable. Bear in mind though, that with these other types of switch the mounting arrangements can be quite awkward. With rocker types in particular, you often have to make a rectangular mounting hole very accurately indeed. Make it just fractionally too small and the switch will not fit into it, or marginally too large and it will not snap into place properly. With the slightest provocation the switch simply drops out the mounting hole.

Sub-miniature toggle switches mostly require a single 6.3 millimetre diameter mounting hole, but the smallest types require 5.2 millimetre diameter mounting holes. Another point to keep in mind is that other types of switch tend to be much larger than sub-miniature toggle types. This can make it difficult to find space for them inside the case, particularly in the case of a small project.

When dealing with switches you will encounter the terms s.p.s.t., s.p.d.t., d.p.s.t., and d.p.d.t. The first of these stands for single pole single throw, and this is the most simple type of switch. It has just two tags, and it is just a simple on/off type switch. A d.p.s.t. switch is a double pole single throw switch. This is basically just two s.p.s.t. switches controlled by a single lever, slider, or whatever. A switch of this type therefore has four tags. An s.p.d.t. switch is a single pole double throw type. This type of switch has three tags. The centre tag connects to one of the other two, depending on the setting of the lever. These are also known as changeover switches, which is a fair description of their function. A d.p.d.t. switch is a double pole double throw switch, and this is two s.p.d.t. switches controlled in unison. This type of switch therefore has six tags. The components lists make it quite clear which type of switch is required.

A heavy-duty push button switch is specified for a few projects. The point of using a switch of this type is that with the project on the floor it can be operated by foot. This permits a 'look no hands' method of control to be used during 'live' performances. Some of the larger component catalogues list one or two heavy-duty push button switches. Ordinary types can be used, but the smaller types should be avoided. They would be awkward in use, and could well have extremely short operating lives. These switches are perfectly satisfactory where a project has an ordinary finger operated push-button control. Heavy-duty push button switches need quite large mounting holes which normally have to be 12.5 millimetres or more in diameter. Small push-button switches almost invariably require a 7 millimetre diameter mounting hole.

A few of the projects require a more complicated type of switch, and these are the 4 way 3 pole and 6 way 2 pole rotary switches used in some of the MIDI projects. These are standard switches which you should find listed in any electronic components catalogue. The only complication is that you might have the choice of 'break-before make' and 'make before break' types. For the projects featured here it is the 'break-before-make' variety that is needed. Rotary switches normally have 10 millimetre diameter mounting bushes and standard 6 millimetre diameter control shafts.

Batteries

The projects featured in this book are mostly powered from 9 volt batteries. Some require 6 or 12 volt battery packs. This helps to keep things simple, and for beginners it keeps things safe. The shock from a 6, 9, or 12 volt battery is so slight that you are totally unaware of it. The shock from the 240 volt mains supply can be lethal. For many of the projects a small (PP3 size) battery is adequate, but with some a higher capacity battery is preferable. I would recommend using six HP7 size cells in one of the plastic battery holders that are available from the larger component retailers. The connection to the holder is made via an ordinary PP3 type battery clip incidentally. Other high capacity 9 volt batteries, such as PP9 size batteries, should also be suitable for the projects which have higher current consumptions. The 6 and 12 volt batteries consist of four or eight HP7 size cells in a plastic battery holder. These are just smaller and larger versions of the 9 volt battery holders.

As most readers will be aware, the battery must be connected the right way round. In the early days of semiconductors the likely result of getting the battery connected the wrong way round, even briefly, was the destruction of all the semiconductors in the circuit. Modern semiconductors are mostly more tolerant of the wrong supply voltage, but some integrated circuits will permit very high supply currents to flow if the supply polarity is incorrect. Even if a device should withstand these high currents, it will quickly overheat and be destroyed. Therefore, be very careful to get the battery clip connected with the right polarity. In the wiring diagrams '+' and '-' signs are used to indicate the battery polarity. The red battery clip lead is the positive (+) one, and the black lead is the negative (-) one.

Stripboard

Photo 1.4 Stripboard used for
construction of these projects
(a) Topside
(b) Underside

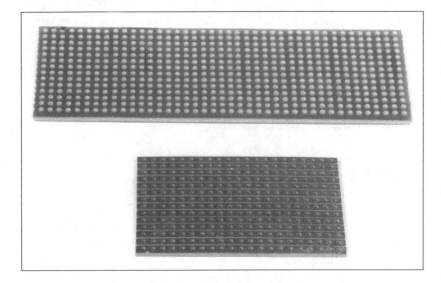

These projects are all based on stripboard, which is a form of proprietary printed circuit board. In some catalogues you may find it listed
under the proprietary name 'Veroboard'. It consists basically of a
piece of thin board which is brown in colour and made from an insulating material. It is drilled with holes on a 0.1 inch matrix, and strips
of copper join up rows of holes. Figure 1.3 shows this general
scheme of things. Something which tends to confuse some beginners
is that the copper side of the board is often referred to as the underside, and the non-copper side is called the top side. It might seem reasonable to assume that the plain side would be called the underside.
However, the components are fitted on the plain side of the board,
which therefore becomes the top side.

Figure 1.3 Stripboard has holes
on a 0.1 inch matrix and rows of
copper strips on one side.

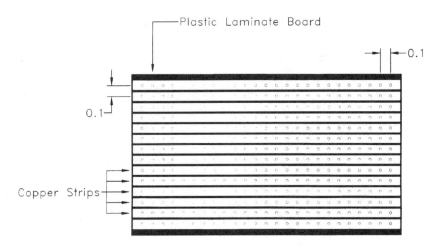

These projects do not use stripboard panels of the standard sizes in which it is normally sold. Therefore, boards of the correct size must be cut from larger pieces using a hacksaw. When cutting the board have the copper side facing upwards. Otherwise the copper strips that are cut might tend to rip away from the board. Cut along rows of holes rather than trying to cut between rows (which is virtually impossible as they are so close together). This leaves rather rough edges, but these can easily be smoothed to a neat finish. Some stripboards seem to be made of a rather brittle material that can easily crack and break when it is being sawn. Always proceed carefully, using minimal force when cutting stripboard.

The component leads are threaded through the appropriate holes on the non-copper side of the board, and the components are pressed hard against the board. The leads are trimmed on the underside of the board using wire clippers, and then soldered to the copper strips. The leads should be trimmed so that about two or three millimetres of wire protrudes on the underside of the board. The solder should then flow nicely over the end of the leadout wire and copper strip to produce a sort of mountain shaped joint, as in Figure 1.4(a).

If you end up with a blob shaped joint, as in Figure 1.4(b), then it is likely that you have a 'dry' joint which is not making a proper electrical connection between the lead and the copper strip. Other tell-tale signs of a bad joint are lots of burnt flux around the joint, and a dull, crazed appearance to the solder instead of the normal shiny finish. If you end up with a suspect joint, it is best to remove the solder, clean up the end of the leadout wire and the copper strip around it using a small file, and then try again.

The most important point to keep in mind when soldering components to a circuit board is that the bit of the iron should be applied to the joint first, and then some solder should be fed in. This gets the joint hot before the solder is applied, which helps the solder to flow over the joint properly. What is definitely the wrong way of tackling this type of joint is to put some solder onto the iron and to then try to apply it to the lead and copper strip. The solder contains cores of flux which help the solder to flow properly over the joint. This flux tends to rapidly burn away if solder is placed on the bit of the iron.

When you try to transfer the solder to the joint there are then two problems. Firstly, with little flux in the solder it will not flow readily over the leadout wire and copper strip. Secondly, the joint has not been pre-heated, which also tends to restrict the flow of the solder. The result is usually a reluctance for the solder to leave the iron, and if it does, it usually just produces a blob on the leadout wire. This gives a joint which is highly unreliable both electrically and physically. Although this may seem to be an easy way of soldering, it is very

I would strongly urge newcomers to electronic project construction to practice soldering on a small piece of stripboard using some pieces of wire and resistors, prior to trying to build their first project. This may seem a bit wasteful, but the cost of the materials used in this exercise will probably be no more than about a pound. It could easily prevent you from wasting several pounds worth of components and a lot of time on a first project which becomes a total failure.

Figure 1.4 A good soldered joint has a mountain shape, as in (a) The blob shape of (b) usually means that a 'dry joint' has been produced.

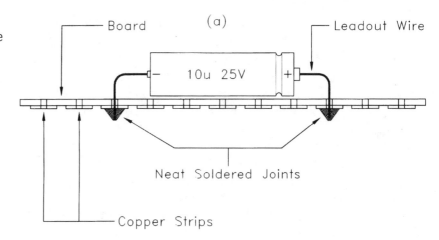

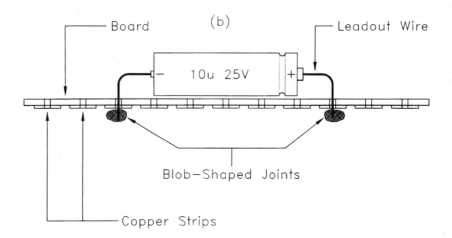

ineffective and should definitely not be used.

Although you should not try to solder in this way, you should place some solder onto the bit of the iron from time to time, so as to always keep the end nicely covered with some reasonably fresh solder. This is known as 'tinning' the bit incidentally. The point of doing this is that it helps to give a good thermal contact between the bit and the joints, which helps to give good quality results.

Soldering iron

It is important to use a suitable soldering iron and type of solder. Any small electric iron should be suitable. By small I mean one that has a rating of somewhere around 15 to 25 watts. There is no need to use something elaborate such as a temperature controlled iron. An ordinary 'no frills' iron will do the job perfectly well. A matching soldering iron stand should be considered an essential extra, not an optional one. For modern electronic work a small bit is required. One of around 2 to 2.5 millimetres in diameter should be suitable. Trying to solder components onto stripboard using an iron fitted with a bit much larger than this can be very difficult indeed. You are likely to find that you have soldered each lead to two or three copper strips!

Types of solder

The solder should be a multi-cored type intended for electrical and electronic work. It is generally available in two thicknesses. The 22 s.w.g. type is the thinner gauge, and is the most useful for building circuit boards. The much thicker 18 s.w.g. solder is better for larger joints, such as when wiring up the controls and sockets. I would not recommend the 18 s.w.g. type for building circuit boards. If you are only going to buy one gauge of solder, then the 22 s.w.g. type is definitely the one to buy. However, it is useful to buy a small amount of the 18 s.w.g. type as well.

Missing links

If you look at the diagrams which show the component sides of the circuit boards, you will notice that there are numerous pairs of holes joined by lines. These lines represent link wires, which are unavoidable when using stripboard with modern components. These wires can in most cases be made from the pieces of wire trimmed from resistor leadout wires. I do not suggest this method of working as an economy measure - the wire used for most resistor leadouts is ideal for use as link wires.

In some cases too many link wires might be needed, or some of the wires might be longer than the available leadout trimmings. The link wires must then be made from some 22 or 24 s.w.g. tinned copper wire. 22 s.w.g. is a bit thicker than is ideal, and 24 s.w.g. is slightly thinner than would be ideal. I find that 24 s.w.g. wire is slightly easier to use than 22 s.w.g. wire, but this is just a personal preference.

It is important that the link wires are quite taut, as there is otherwise a risk of short circuits occurring. I find the best way of fitting them is to first solder one end of the link in place. Then thread the other end of the wire through the appropriate hole in the board, pull it tight using some pliers, trim it to length on the underside of the board, and then solder it in place. If you want to make absolutely certain that no short circuits to any link wires occur, simply fit pieces of p.v.c. sleeving over them. However, I have never found it necessary to do this provided the link wires are made reasonably taut.

Wiring-up

In most projects there is a certain amount of wiring from the circuit board to off-board components, such as switches, sockets, potentiometers, etc. There may also be some wiring from one off-board component to another. This is generally known by such names as 'hard wiring', 'spaghetti wiring', and 'point-to-point wiring'. Whatever your preferred term, it is normally completed using thin multi-strand wire. Something like 7/0.2 (i.e. seven cores of 0.2 millimetre diameter wire), p.v.c. insulated wire is suitable. This, or something similar, should be found in any electronics component catalogue. It will probably be described as 'hook- up' wire or 'connecting' wire. Single core wire, which is also known as solid core wire, is less than ideal for most hard wiring. It is not very flexible, and unless used very carefully it has a tendency to break.

I often use ribbon cable for wiring up projects. Ribbon cable is a multi-way cable that consists of what are effectively several pieces of multi-strand p.v.c. insulated connecting wire laid side-by-side. The wires are fixed together by an overall covering of transparent plastic. It lives up to its name as this type of cable is flat and ribbon- like. It is available as a single coloured (usually grey) cable, or as multi-coloured 'rainbow' cable. The latter is better for wiring-up purposes as having each lead a different colour makes it easy to tell which lead is which. This cable is available from 10 way to about 50 way cable. For our present purposes any ribbon cable will do, but ten way cable is probably the most practical choice.

Usually when you are wiring-up a project you will find that there is not a single wire running from the component panel to an off-board component. In most cases there are two, three, or four leads running from the circuit board to each off-board component. There would normally be three leads in the case of a potentiometer for example. In order to help keep things as neat as possible, the circuit boards are designed so that, as far as reasonably possible, all the leads that go to an off-board component emanate from the same area of the board.

When wiring-up a project using ordinary hook-up wire you can make things neater by tying together the wires in each group. Ribbon cable represents an easier way of obtaining the same effect. If you have three leads running from the board to an off-board component, first break away a three way cable from the main piece of ribbon cable, and then cut off a suitable length. This can then be used to provide the three connections to the off-board component. No cable tying is required, as the leads are already held together as a single cable.

A small piece of insulation must be removed from the end of each lead before it can be connected to the tag of an off-board component. It is important to use a pair of wire strippers to do this. You can remove the insulation using scissors, a penknife, etc., but you could easily end up injuring yourself. Also, you are likely to damage the wire, which will then fatigue easily, and is likely to snap before too long. Wire strippers enable the insulation to be removed quickly and easily, and they can be adjusted so that they will cut just the right depth into the insulation, leaving the wires unharmed.

Making connections to off-board components requires a slightly different method of soldering to the one described previously. First, it is important to tin the ends of the leads and the tags of the components with a generous amount of solder. In most cases you will find that the leads and tags take the solder without any difficulty, but some may not. This will be due to dirt or corrosion, which can be scraped away using a miniature file or the blade of a small penknife. Once the tinning has been completed, hook the end of the lead through and around the hole in the appropriate component tag. Then apply the iron and some solder in the normal way, and a good strong joint should be produced. Some component tags are actually pins which lack the hole. With these you simply hook the wire around the pin, and then solder it in place in the normal way.

At the component panel end of the hard wiring you could connect the leads direct to the stripboard. This tends to be a rather awkward way of going about matters, and is also unreliable. The wires tend to break away from the board and the pieces of strip to which they are connected.

A better way of tackling things is to use solder pins at the points on the board where connections to off-board components must be made. For 0.1 inch stripboard it is the 1 millimetre diameter pins that are required. There are single and double sided pins, but for the projects featured here you will probably only need the single sided type. These are inserted from the copper side of the board, and pushed home so that very little is left protruding on the underside of the board. A tool for fitting solder pins is available, but they can usually be pushed into place properly with the aid of some pliers. Use a generous amount of solder when connecting the pins to the copper strips, and also tin the tops of the pins with liberal amount of solder. There should then be no difficulty in connecting the leads to them

Mounting tension

There are three basic methods of mounting completed component panels inside cases. The most simple is to mount the board in the guide rails that are moulded into many plastic cases, and a few aluminium types. This is only possible if the board is made of a size that will fit into the guide rails with a fair degree of precision. This method is not applicable to most of the projects featured in this book, although it might be possible in some instances if the board is made larger than is really necessary, so that it will fit the guide rails properly.

My preferred method is to simply bolt the board in place using 6BA nuts and bolts. If your supplier sells only metric sizes, M3 is the nearest metric equivalent to 6BA. Whichever of these you use, 3.3 millimetre diameter mounting holes are suitable. It is important to use spacers about 5 to 10 millimetres long over the mounting bolts, between the case and the component panel. Alternatively, some extra nuts can be used as spacers. If you are using a metal case these will hold the connections on the underside of the board clear of the metal case, so that they do not short circuit through it.

Whatever type of case you use, the spacers will prevent the board from buckling slightly as the mounting nuts are tightened. This buckling occurs because the underside of the board is far from flat once the components have been added, and there are soldered joints protruding on the underside of the board. If you omit the spacers, it is quite possible that the board will buckle so badly that it will crack, or even break into several pieces.

The final method is to use the special plastic stand-offs that are available from most electronic component retailers. These vary somewhat in design, but the most simple type clip into the case and then the board is clipped onto them. The holes in the case and the board must be drilled very accurately if this type of stand-off is to work properly. With the stand-offs of this type that I have used, they never really seemed to hold the board in place properly. There is an alternative type which is mounted on the case via self-tapping screws, and this seems to be more reliable. However, with stripboard I much prefer to have the component panels securely bolted to the case.

Layout

There is a vast range of project cases available these days, from inexpensive plastic boxes through to elaborate metal instrument cases which, if used for most projects, would account for more than 50% of the overall cost. There is no one case which is suitable for all the projects in this book. The projects cover various types and complexities, and whereas a cheap plastic box might be appropriate to one project, another might require a larger metal case. Where appropriate, the text gives some guidance as to the best type and size of case for each project. The size of the component panel will give you a good idea of the minimum size of case that is needed.

When designing the overall layout of a project you need to give some thought to how the unit will be used. For instance, do not have sockets too close to, or immediately above control knobs. It is very easy to produce a front panel layout that looks very neat and plausible, but when you plug in the input and output leads the plugs get in the way and make it virtually impossible to adjust some of the controls.

In general it is best to keep inputs well separated from outputs. This is more important with some projects than with others. In the worst cases, having an input socket anywhere near to the output socket is almost certain to render the circuit unstable, possibly preventing it from working at all. Fortunately, none of the projects featured here is as pernickety as this. Try to avoid layouts that result in lots of crossed-over wires when you wire-up the project. This is not just a matter of making the interior of the project look neat. Long leads trailing all over the place can reduce the performance of a circuit or cause instability. Also, if there should be a problem with the project at some time, fault finding will be much easier if the wiring is neat, tidy, and easy to follow.

The right order

This covers the basics of project construction, and should tell you most of what you need to know. The rest can be learned from looking through one or two large component catalogues, and from experience. A summary of the basic steps in building a project is provided below. This list has the steps in the order that I would suggest you go about things. Not everyone would totally agree with this, and you might prefer to do things your own way in due course, but this gives you a sound initial method of working.

1   Order all the components you need, being careful to get the right ones (including the right types of capacitor etc.).
2   Once you have all the components, identify them all, and check that you have been supplied with the correct parts.
3   Cut the stripboard to size and drill the mounting holes.
4   Fit the components and link wires to the board. Start at one end and work your way methodically to the other side of the board. Fit the solder pins, but do not put the integrated circuits in their holders yet.
5   Work out the case layout, and drill all the holes.
6   Fit the controls and sockets in the case, and then fit the component panel.
7   Wire-up the project using hook-up wire or pieces of ribbon cable.
8   Fit the integrated circuits in their holders.
9   Check the wiring etc., and when all is well, switch on and test the project..

Testing

If a project fails to work, and you do not have the necessary technical skills and equipment to check it properly, all is not lost. The problem could be due to a faulty component, but in all honesty this is highly unlikely provided you buy new components from any respectable supplier. There are many 'bargain packs' of components on offer, and some of these represent outstanding value for money. Others, with the best will in the world, have to be regarded as bags of rubbish. Without technical expertise and some test equipment it is not possible to sort out the good from the bad. Therefore, it is advisable for beginners to use only new components of good quality.

Even if you use top quality components from one of the larger retailers it is obviously still possible that a faulty component could slip through. This is extremely rare though, since components undergo quite stringent testing. Where a faulty component is supplied it is usually due to it having sustained physical damage somewhere along the line. This damage, such as a missing leadout wire, will almost invariably be obvious when you examine the newly obtained components. At one time there were companies selling semiconductors of dubious quality. Some of these were not quite what they purported to be, while others were so-called 'genuine duds' that failed to work at all. Fortunately, this practice seemed to die out some years ago. Any semiconductors you buy will almost certainly be the 'real thing' from one of the main semiconductor manufacturers.

Problems are unlike to be due to faulty components, but it is a good idea to visually inspect the board for signs of damaged compo-

Photo 1.5
A Modern digital multimeters can measure a wide range of electrical quantities and test many types of component
B Even a simple analogue multimeter is invaluable for continuity checks etc. when you are faced with an inoperative project

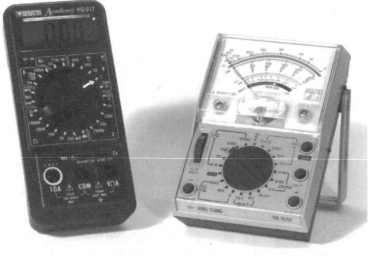

A   B

nents. Are there any discoloured components which overheated when you took too long to solder them into circuit? Are there other signs of damage, such as a polyester capacitor that is parting company with one of its leadout wires? Replace any suspect looking components.

The wrong component rather than a faulty component is a much more likely cause of problems. Check the circuit board carefully against the diagrams and components list, making sure that the right parts are in the right places. With stripboard construction you need to be very careful not to get one or two of the leadout wires connected to the wrong copper strip. Are the electrolytic capacitors and semiconductors fitted the right way round? You are unlikely to miss out a component, as you would presumably notice that there was one left over. Link wires are a different matter though. Check that there are the same number of link wires on the component layout diagram and on the circuit board.

Probably the most likely area for faults is on the underside of the board. Did you place the solder on the bit of the iron and then transfer it to the joint? This virtually guarantees bad joints, but is the method that many beginners seem to insist on adopting. If there are any suspect joints, remove the solder from them, clean up the copper strip and leadout wire by scraping then with the blade of a penknife, and try again using the correct method of soldering (as described previously in this chapter). When inspecting the underside of the board look out for joints that are globular in appearance, solder that has a dull rather than a shiny surface, and joints that are covered with burned and black flux. These often mean that the joint concerned is something less than perfect.

Another point to check is that the breaks in the copper strips are all present and in the right places. If you find that a break has been made in the wrong place, simply solder a piece of wire over the break and make a new one in the right place. Look carefully at each break to determine whether or not it has been fully cut though. On several occasions I have found that a newly constructed project has failed to work due to a minute trail of copper bridging what should be a break in a copper strip. These are sometimes so thin that they are barely visible with the naked eye. A magnifying glass is more than slightly helpful when inspecting the underside of a stripboard.

With stripboard construction the main cause of faults is short circuits between adjacent copper strips due to minute blobs of excess solder. The copper strips are so close together that it is very easy to solder across two strips. This will often be quite obvious, as the strips will be bridged over a length of several millimetres. Sometimes though, there may be only a very fine trail of solder which is barely visible. Once again, a magnifying glass is very helpful when making a

Tech tip
A technique which I have found quite useful is to carefully score between each pair of copper strips using a sharp modelling knife. If there are any solder trails which are so small that they are defeating your eyesight, this treatment should cut through them and remove the problem. Some years ago when I was making large numbers of projects on stripboard I found that this method was successful in curing a surprisingly large percentage of ailing circuit boards.

visual inspection of the copper side of the board. Even with an aid to vision, some solder trails can be very difficult to locate. Cleaning the underside of the board with one of the special cleaners that are available can help matters. Look especially carefully at areas of the board where there are a lot of soldered joints.

Simple MIDI tester

The basic idea is to unplug the MIDI lead from the 'IN' socket of a device that is not responding to the master unit, and to connect to this device instead. If sending MIDI messages to the tester results in its LED indicator operating, you know that the master unit is probably functioning correctly, and that the MIDI lead is in good working order. The fault is either in the slave unit, or something in the system is not set up correctly (the master and slave units could be set to different MIDI channels for example). If the indicator LED does not operate, then the fault is either in the master unit or the MIDI cable.

It has to be admitted that this tester provides only a very limited amount of information when tracking down problems with a MIDI system. However, it is very inexpensive to build, and is a piece of gear I have found to be quite useful in practice. The next two sections of this book deal with more sophisticated testers that provide more comprehensive information, such as the received message types and (where appropriate) their channel numbers.

Circuit operation

Figure 2.1 shows the circuit diagram for the simple MIDI tester. In order to conform to the MIDI hardware standard it is a requirement

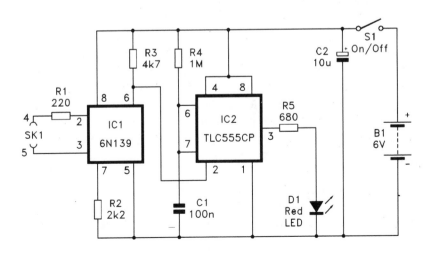

Figure 2.1 The circuit diagram for the simple MIDI tester. D1 flashes each time a message is received

that all inputs should have electrical isolation provided by an opto-isolator. This electrical isolation helps to avoid problems with 'hum' loops, and with noise being coupled from a digital control device (computer, sequencer, etc.) to the audio stages of instruments. In the current application the isolation is of no real advantage, since there are no audio stages to pick-up digital noise or mains 'hum'. It is still necessary to include the isolation though, as it is important that the tester 'looks' to the master unit just like every other piece of MIDI equipment. Otherwise there is a slight risk that the tester would work with slightly faulty devices which would not drive other MIDI devices properly.

A basic opto-isolator consists of an infra-red LED which has its light output directed at a phototransistor. These two components are housed in an opaque case that shields the phototransistor from any ambient light. In most applications, including the present one, the phototransistor is used as a simple switch. With the LED switched off the phototransistor passes only minute leakage currents, and is also switched off. Passing a current of a few milliamps through the LED results in it shining a significant amount of light onto the phototransistor which then passes much higher leakage currents. This effectively switches on the phototransistor, giving much the same result as if it had been switched on by a base current.

In a MIDI context there are two problems in using a basic opto-isolator. One is simply that the efficiency tends to be quite low, with a current flow on the output side that is only a fraction of the input current. The latter is about 5 milliamps for MIDI equipment incidentally. The second problem is that opto-isolators are very slow devices by electronic standards. Although MIDI is not very demanding in this respect, most opto-isolators can not switch quite fast enough to couple a MIDI signal properly.

The opto-isolator used in this project is a 6N139 (IC1). On the output side of this device there is a photodiode driving an emitter follower stage, which in turn drives a common emitter switching transistor. This diode plus two transistor amplifier provides both improved efficiency and a much faster switching speed. Efficiencies of several hundred percent are easily achieved, and the switching speed is in line with the requirements laid down in the MIDI hardware specification. R1 is a current limiting resistor on the input side of IC1, and R2 is the discrete load resistor for the emitter follower stage on the output side of IC1. R3 is the load resistor for the open collector output transistor.

The circuit would provide the required function if R3 was simply replaced with the indicator LED and a current limiting resistor. One problem with this approach is that it would not give very good LED brightness. The pulses of current through the LED would usually be very brief and intermittent, giving a low average LED current.

Improved results are obtained by using IC2 to act as a pulse stretcher. IC2 is a low power 555 timer device which is used here as a simple monostable. Each time a MIDI message is received, the trigger input at pin 2 of IC2 is taken low. This results in IC2 producing an output pulse having a duration which is controlled by the values of R4 and C1. With the specified values an output pulse of just over one tenth of a second is obtained at pin 3 of IC2. This operates D1 for long enough to ensure that a clear indication is provided. Note that if a string of MIDI messages are received in rapid succession, IC2 will be retriggered almost immediately each time an output pulse ends. D1 may then appear to light almost continuously.

The current consumption of the circuit is extremely low under standby conditions, and will probably be only a fraction of a milliamp. The current drain is much higher while the LED is operating, and it is then about 6 milliamps. This is still low enough to give an extremely long battery life.

Construction

Figure 2.2 shows the component layout for the stripboard panel, while Figure 2.3 shows the underside (copper side) of the board. The arrowheads at one corner of the board show how the board has been turned over. The hard wiring is provided in Figure 2.4 (which should be used in conjunction with Figure 2.2). A board having 26 holes by 16 copper strips is needed. The principles of stripboard construction are covered in detail in Chapter 1.

Although a TLC555CP is specified for IC2, this circuit should work perfectly well using any low power version of the 555 timer (L555, ICM7555, etc.). It will also work using the standard version, but this will give a much higher current consumption, and greatly reduced battery life. Although the low power versions of the 555 mostly make use of CMOS technology, the built-in protection circuits render anti-static handling precautions unnecessary.

This unit will fit into most small plastic or metal project boxes, but a few have insufficient depth to accommodate the battery pack. This consists of four HP7 size cells fitted in a plastic battery holder. The case needs an internal depth of about 30 millimetres in order to house this properly. Connections to the battery holder are made via an ordinary PP3 style battery clip.

Figure 2.2 The stripboard component layout for the simple MIDI tester

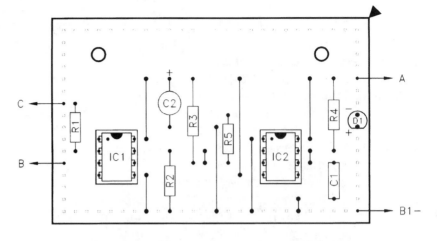

Figure 2.3 The underside of the stripboard panel. The board has 26 holes by 16 strips

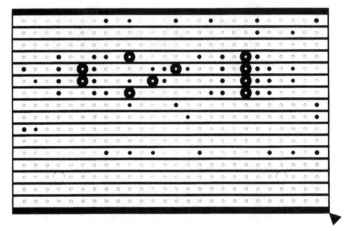

User tips

The best way to check that the unit is functioning correctly is to connect it to the output of a keyboard instrument via a standard MIDI cable. Switch on the tester and then play a few notes on the keyboard. The LED should flash each time a key is pressed, and again when the note is released. If the keyboard has aftertouch, holding down a key should produce a lot of activity from the LED indicator. Remember that the LED may appear to light continuously if there is a lot of MIDI activity. This unit is useful for checking to see just what does and what does not result in a MIDI device transmitting messages. Try operating the modulation wheels, the push buttons that control program changes, MIDI modes, etc., to determine which ones produce MIDI activity. Many MIDI devices have built-in filtering which enables certain types of MIDI message to be switched off. This unit can be used to check if the transmission of certain MIDI messages has indeed been switched off. Simply operate the appropriate control or controls, and check that the LED indicator does not operate.

Components (Simple MIDI tester)

Resistor (all 0.25 watt 5% carbon film)

R1   220R
R2   2k2
R3   4k7
R4   1M
R5   680R

Capacitors

C1   100n polyester
C2   10u 25V radial elect

Semiconductors

IC1   6N139 opto-isolator
IC2   TLC555CP or similar
D1   Red panel mounting LED

Miscellaneous

SK1   5 way (180 degree) DIN socket
S1   s.p.s.t. min toggle switch
B1   6 volt (four HP7 size cells in plastic holder)
       0.1 inch stripboard 26 holes by 16 copper strips
       Small plastic or metal case
       8 pin DIL i.c. holder (2 off)
       PP3 size battery connector

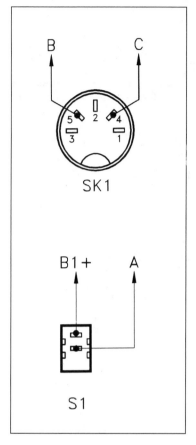

Figure 2.4 Details of the small amount of hard wiring

③ Message grabber

T his project is another MIDI checker, but it is much more sophisticated than the unit described previously. It does not simply tell you whether or not messages are being received, but instead it decodes the first message received so that you can check that the message type is as expected. In the case of a channel message the unit also indicates the channel number of the received message.

What the unit actually does is to grab the header byte of the first message that is received, and it then displays the data in raw binary form on an eight LED display. In order to understand the results produced by this unit it is more than a little helpful to have a basic understanding of the way in which MIDI messages are coded. On the other hand, it is not absolutely essential to understand MIDI in this sort of depth, since you can simply compare the results obtained against the tables provided.

In reality it will probably be necessary to do this at first anyway, since it is difficult to remember the binary codes for all the MIDI messages. However, after using the unit for a while you will probably find that you recognise the binary patterns for the more common messages. Similarly, with a little practice there is little difficulty in converting the four bit binary codes into their corresponding channel numbers.

Photograph of completed message grabber

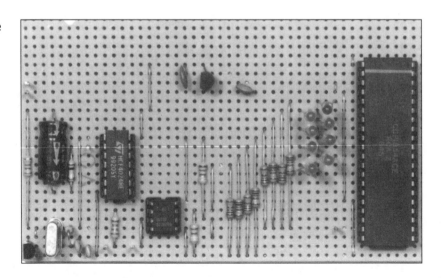

When a MIDI message is sent from one device to another, all that is actually being sent is a series of numbers in the range 0 to 255. A rigid method of coding is used so that every MIDI device will properly decode received messages, and where appropriate will respond to them in the correct manner. There is a slight complication in that the numbers themselves are in binary form. They are eight digit binary numbers (bytes), and with the binary system each digit is a '0' or a '1'. The numbers therefore run from 00000000 (0 decimal) to 11111111 (255 decimal). This may seem to be a rather crude way of doing things, which it is, but it is currently the only practical way of handling things. It is a system that the hardware can easily accommodate, since the '0's and '1's can be easily represented using a very low voltage and a higher voltage respectively.

All MIDI messages contain a header byte which tells the receiving devices the message type (note on, note off, etc.), and in the case of channel messages it also indicates the channel number for the message. Most MIDI messages also have one or more data bytes which follow the header byte. These indicate such things as which note should be switched on or off, and how loudly each note should be played. Here we are concerned only with header bytes, which are normally of prime importance when trouble shooting on MIDI systems.

For the purposes of MIDI header byte coding, the eight bits of binary information are split into two halves. In the slightly zany world of computers, half a byte is inevitably known as a 'nibble'. One nibble of a header byte (the four left hand bits) indicates the message type. The other nibble carries the channel number. The system of coding is different for system messages, which do not have channel numbers. They are directed to all the pieces of equipment in the system, regardless of what channel or channels they are operating on. The left hand nibble contains the code for system messages, while the right hand nibble indicates the message type (clock, song position pointer, etc.). This tester will therefore indicate the message type for both system and channel messages, and the channel number for system messages. It is probably the channel number that is of most value when MIDI troubleshooting, since incorrect channelling is a frequent cause of problems.

Circuit operation

Refer to Figure 3.1 for the full circuit diagram of the Message Grabber project. IC2 is an opto-isolator which converts the MIDI input signal into a form that can drive IC3 correctly. IC3 is a complex

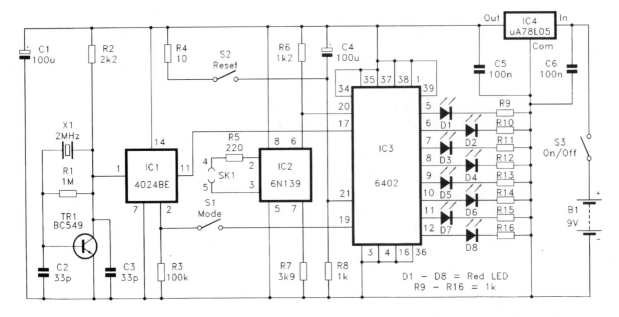

Figure 3.1 The circuit diagram for the message grabber. IC3 is the UART which is central to the operation of the circuit

device of a type known as a UART (universal asynchronous receiver/transmitter). MIDI is a form of serial interface, which means that the eight bits of information in each byte are not sent via eight separate wires. Instead, they are sent over one wire (plus an earth lead), on what is literally a bit-by-bit basis. The purpose of the UART is to convert the incoming serial signal back into eight bit parallel data which appears on its eight outputs. In this case these outputs are pins 5 to 12 of IC3. As its name implies, a UART can also convert parallel data on eight inputs to a stream of serial data on a single output. The transmission facility is not utilized in this circuit, but it is used in the MIDI pedal projects which are featured later in this book.

MIDI is a form of asynchronous serial interface, which simply means that no synchronisation signal of any kind is provided using an additional interconnection. Instead, simple synchronisation signals are sent together with each byte of data. This system works very reliably, but only if both ends of the system are designed to send/receive data at the same rate. The rate for MIDI interfaces is 31250 baud, or 31250 bits per second in other words. The baud rate of IC3 is controlled by an external clock oscillator which must provide a signal at sixteen times the required baud rate. This works out at 500000Hz (500kHz) in this case. TR1 is used as the basis of a crystal oscillator which operates at 2MHz. IC1 is a seven stage binary divider, but in this case only two stages are used. These divide the 2MHz signal by four to give the required 500kHz clock signal for IC3.

Serial interfaces use a variety of word formats. These formats differ in the number of bits sent in each group, the exact nature of the synchronisation signals added to each group, and whether or not a simple method of error checking is implemented. MIDI uses the most common word format of one start bit, eight data bits, one stop bit, and no parity checking. A UART can handle any normal word format, including the one used in MIDI interfacing. It is simply a matter of connecting pins 34 to 39 to the appropriate supply rails in order to program the device to operate with the required word format.

Each of IC3's eight parallel outputs drives a LED indicator via a current limiting resistor. Each time a new byte of data is received, the new binary pattern is fed to the outputs, and the appropriate LEDs then switch on until the next byte is received. With S1 in the open position, the unit will operate in this free-running mode. It is of limited value when used in this way, since the bytes of data will normally be received at such a high rate that the LEDs will appear to flash in a more or less random fashion. In the free-running mode this circuit is really little more than a simple MIDI checker of the type described previously.

With S1 closed, a status output of IC3 is connected through to the reset input of IC1. This status output goes high each time a fresh byte of data has been received, decoded, and placed onto the parallel output lines. As soon as the first byte of MIDI information has been received, this output therefore goes high and resets IC1. By holding IC1 in the reset state the clock signal to IC3 is blocked, and it is 'frozen' with the first MIDI byte on its outputs. C4 and R8 provide a reset pulse to IC3 at switch-on, which is essential if IC3 is to initialise properly. S2 can be operated briefly in order to manually provide a reset pulse to IC3. Doing so returns pin 19 of IC3 to the low state so that the unit is made ready to grab the next MIDI byte that is received.

The circuit requires a reasonably accurate and well stabilised 5 volt supply. This is derived from a 9 volt battery via a small monolithic voltage regulator (IC4). The basic current consumption of the circuit is only a few milliamps, but about three milliamps per active LED must be added to this. The current consumption can therefore be as much as about 30 milliamps with all eight LEDs switched on. A fairly high capacity battery is therefore needed, such as six HP7 size cells.

Construction

Details of the component layout, underside of the stripboard, and point-to-point wiring are provided in Figures 3.2 to 3.4 respectively. The board measure 51 holes by 30 copper strips. Construction of the board is reasonably straightforward, but with a board as large and

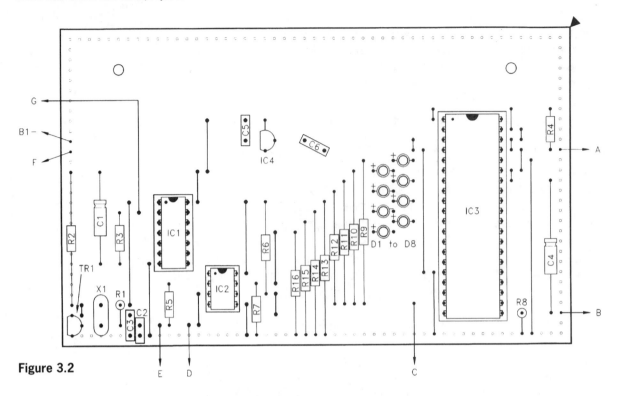

Figure 3.2

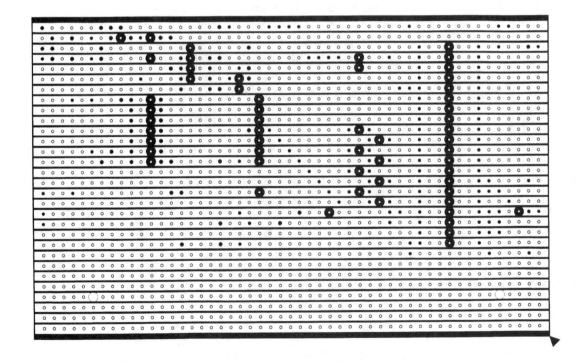

Figure 3.3

well populated as this it is essential to proceed carefully and methodically. IC1 and IC3 are both CMOS integrated circuits, and as such they require the normal anti-static handling precautions. IC3 can be a 6402, an AY-3-1015D, or any direct equivalent to these. Crystal X1 should be a wire-ended type that can be soldered direct onto the board. The bit of the iron should be kept on each soldered joint no longer than is really necessary when connecting this component, as excessive heat can damage the internal mounting of the crystal.

I used miniature (3 millimetres in diameter) red LEDs mounted direct on the circuit board. Using this method, the LEDs must be left with long leads, and the circuit board is mounted close behind the front panel of the case. The LED display then fits into eight small holes drilled at suitable positions in the front panel. The alternative is to have the LEDs mounted off-board, and to hard wire them to the board. This enables panel LEDs of any desired size and shape to be used, but with some sixteen connections to be made to the display it requires a lot of awkward hard wiring.

The six HP7 size cells fit into a plastic battery holder, and the connections to the holder are made via an ordinary PP3 type battery clip. Any fairly high capacity 9 volt battery should suffice, such as a PP9 size, but note that most of the larger 9 volt batteries require large type battery connectors. These are usually in the form of separate positive and negative connectors. A PP3 battery might be adequate as the power source, but only if the unit is likely to receive brief and very intermittent use.

Opposite:

Figure 3.2 The stripboard component layout for the message grabber. The board has 51 holes by 30 strips

Figure 3.3 The underside of the stripboard panel

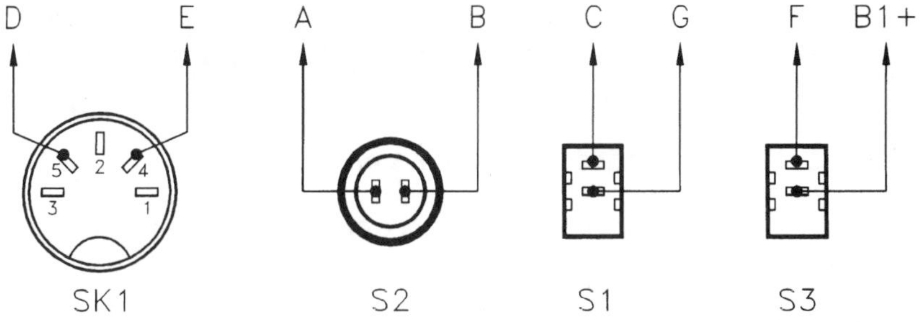

Figure 3.4 Details of the hard wiring for the message grabber

User tips

The LED display could adopt any pattern at switch-on, but it is most likely that all the LEDs will switch on, or they will all remain off. When initially testing the unit it is best to start with it set to the free-running mode (S1 set open). Connect the input of the unit to the MIDI output of a keyboard instrument, and play some notes, operate the modulation wheel, etc. to check that the LED display responds to each burst of MIDI action. Then switch to the single-shot mode (S1 closed), and play a note on the keyboard. The binary code for a note on message is 1001. Accordingly, D1 and D4 should switch on, while D2 and D3 should switch off. The states of D5 to D8 depend on the channel used. For initial testing try channel 2. This will result in D8 switching on, and D5 to D7 switching off. Remember that once a byte of data has been latched onto the display, the reset button must be pressed before the unit will 'grab' another byte.

For all MIDI header bytes the most significant bit is set to 1, which means that for all types of message D1 should be switched on. If D1 is off after a message has been 'grabbed', either the device sending the messages is faulty, or the unit has somehow managed to 'grab' a data byte. These always have the most significant bit set to 0 incidentally. The other three bits in the most significant nibble indicate the message type, which means that it is D2 to D4 of this unit that indicate the message type. There are eight different sets of states for these LEDs, and the appropriate message type for each one is shown in Table 1.

For channel messages the channel number is indicated by D5 to D8, and Table 2 shows the LED states for each channel number. Note that the binary values in the channel number nibble are from 0000 to 1111, which is equivalent of 0 to 15 in decimal, but the convention is to have MIDI channel numbers from 1 to 16. Consequently, the channel number is one more than the binary value in the least significant nibble. This has been taken into account in Table 2.

Finally, for system messages, D2 to D4 show the system message code, and D5 to D8 indicate the message type. Table 3 shows the LED states for some common system messages.

Table 1, Message codes (D1 is always on)

D2	D3	D4	Message type
Off	Off	Off	Note off
Off	Off	On	Note on
Off	On	Off	Polyphonic key pressure
Off	On	On	Control change
On	Off	Off	Program change
On	Off	On	Overall key pressure
On	On	Off	Pitch wheel
On	On	On	System message

Table 2, Channel numbers

D5	D6	D7	D8	Channel number
Off	Off	Off	Off	1
Off	Off	Off	On	2
Off	Off	On	Off	3
Off	Off	On	On	4
Off	On	Off	Off	5
Off	On	Off	On	6
Off	On	On	Off	7
Off	On	On	On	8
On	Off	Off	Off	9
On	Off	Off	On	10
On	Off	On	Off	11
On	Off	On	On	12
On	On	Off	Off	13
On	On	Off	On	14
On	On	On	Off	15
On	On	On	On	16

Table 3, System messages

D5	D6	D7	D8	Message type
Off	Off	Off	Off	Start system exclusive
Off	Off	On	Off	Song position
Off	Off	On	On	Song select
Off	On	On	On	End system exclusive
On	Off	Off	Off	Clock signal
On	Off	On	Off	Start
On	Off	On	On	Continue
On	On	Off	Off	Stop
On	On	On	Off	Active sensing
On	On	On	On	System reset

Components (Message grabber)

Resistors (all 0.25% watt 5% carbon film)

R1	1M
R2	2k2
R3	100k
R4	10R
R5	220R
R6	1k2
R7	3k9
R8 - R16	1k

Capacitors

C1	100u 10V axial elect
C2	33p ceramic plate
C3	33p ceramic plate
C4	100u 10V axial elect
C5	100n ceramic
C6	100n ceramic

Semiconductors

IC1	4024BE
IC2	6N139 opto-isolator
IC3	6402 or equivalent
IC4	uA78L05 (5V 100mA positive regulator)
TR1	BC549
D1 to D8	3mm red LEDs (8 off, see text)

Miscellaneous

S1	s.p.s.t. min toggle switch
S2	Push to make, non-locking push button switch
S3	s.p.s.t. min toggle switch
B1	9 volt (6 x HP7 cells in holder)
SK1	5 way 180 degree DIN socket
X1	2MHz crystal, HC-49/U case
	0.1 inch stripboard 51 holes by 30 strips
	Medium size metal or plastic box
	8 pin DIL i.c. holder
	14 pin DIL i.c. holder
	40 pin DIL i.c. holder
	PP3 type battery connector

Byte grabber | 4

T his project is an extended version of the message grabber described in the previous chapter of this book. Its basic function is the same, but it is not restricted to 'grabbing' the first byte in a sequence. It can be set to 'grab' anything from the first to the sixth byte that is received after the unit has been switched on or reset. This makes the unit very much more versatile, since it is not restricted to displaying header bytes. It can also be used to check any data bytes that follow a header byte.

Most MIDI messages contain a header byte followed by one or two data bytes. Taking a note on message as an example, the header byte is followed by two data bytes. The first of these is the note number, and the second is the velocity byte (i.e. a value indicating how hard the note was played). If the unit is set to 'grab' the third byte and it is fed with a note on message, it will therefore display the velocity data byte. This can be useful for checking whether a keyboard instrument provides a full range of velocity values, or only has about half a dozen different velocity levels. Being able to select anything up to the sixth byte in a sequence means that it is easy to select a byte in the note off section of an note on/off sequence. It is also possible to select bytes from a key pressure message (which are only produced after note on types).

It is important to remember that MIDI data bytes contain only seven bit values. This is because the most significant bit is always set to 1 in header bytes, and to 0 in data bytes, so that receiving devices can easily distinguish between the two types. This means that the range of data values is from 0000000 (0) to 1111111 (127). Therefore, D1 will always be switched off when a data byte is displayed.

Finally assembled byte grabber

Circuit operation

Figure 4.1 shows the full circuit diagram for the byte grabber project. This is much the same as the circuit for the message grabber
project, but it has additional stages based on TR2 and IC4. TR2 is a
simple inverter stage, and it is driven from the status output of IC3
that goes high when a fresh byte of data has been received and placed
on the eight output lines. It drives an input that must be taken low in
order to reset the status output. Each time a byte is received the status output immediately resets itself. The result of this is a brief pulse
at the collector of TR2 each time a fresh byte of data is supplied to
the LEDs.

Figure 4.1 Circuit diagram for the
byte grabber

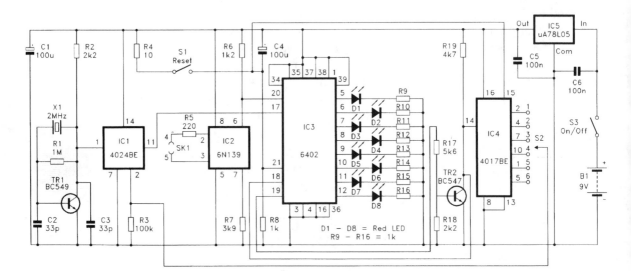

IC4 is a one-of-ten decoder, which is a simple form of counter
circuit. It has ten outputs which are numbered from '0' to '9'. At any
time, only one output is at logic 1 (high), and all the others are at
logic 0 (low). IC4 is reset at switch-on, and this results in output '0'
going high. On the first input pulse output '1' goes high, output '2'
goes high on the next input pulse, and so on until output '9' goes high
on the ninth input pulse. In this case only outputs from '1' to '6' are
used, and one of these is connected to the reset input of IC1 via S2.
When the selected output goes high, the clock signal to IC3 is cut off,
and the display is 'frozen'. Output '1' 'freezes' the display on the first
byte, output '2' 'freezes' it on the second byte, and so on. A free-running mode could be obtained by using a seven way switch for S2,
with the extra way leaving the reset input of IC1 connected through
to nothing. However, such a facility would be largely superfluous on
this more sophisticated version of the grabber.

Construction

Figures 4.2 to 4.4 provide details of the component panel and wiring. The board has 63 holes by 30 copper strips. The notes on construction of the Message Grabber project apply equally to this unit. In addition, note that IC4 is a CMOS device which requires the standard anti-static protection measures. The wiring to S2 can be carried via a

Figure 4.2 Stripboard layout for byte grabber

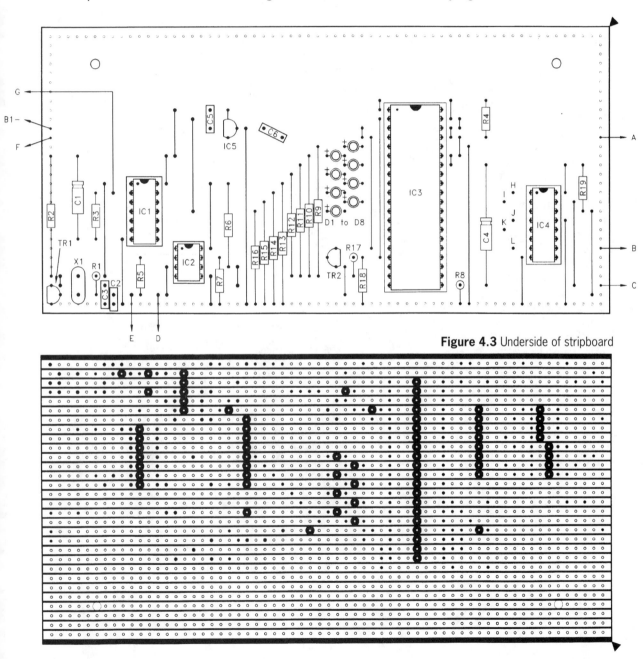

Figure 4.3 Underside of stripboard

Figure 4.4 External wiring for byte grabber

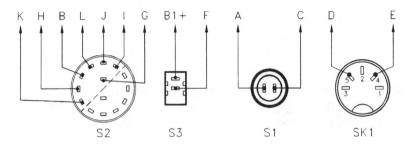

six way ribbon cable, plus a separate lead to carry the connection from point 'G' to point 'G'. S2 is a standard 6 way 2 pole switch, but in this case only one pole is required. The tags of the switch will probably be marked from '1' to '12', plus 'A' and 'B' for the pole tags. It is only tag 'A' and tags from '1' to '6' that are used in this circuit.

Components (Byte grabber)

User tips

The unit is used in much the same way as the message grabber unit, but S2 can be used to select something other than the header byte of the first message. When initially testing the unit connect it to a keyboard instrument, and try S2 at the '1' position to ensure that the unit is 'grabbing' the first byte correctly. Then reset the unit and select position '2' of S2. Next play middle C on the keyboard instrument. This should result in the note value being displayed, and middle C has a note value of 60. This is 0111100 in binary, which means that D3 to D6 should be switched on, and the other four LEDs should be switched off.

Resistors (all 0.25% watt 5% carbon film)

R1	1M
R2	2k2
R3	100k
R4	10R
R5	220R
R6	1k2
R7	3k9
R8 - R16	1k
R17	5k6
R18	2k2
R19	4k7

Capacitors

C1	100u 10V axial elect
C2	33p ceramic plate
C3	33p ceramic plate
C4	100u 10V axial elect
C5	100n ceramic
C6	100n ceramic

Semiconductors

IC1	4024BE
IC2	6N139 opto-isolator
IC3	6402 or equivalent
IC4	4017
IC5	uA78L05 (5V 100mA positive regulator)
TR1	BC549
TR2	BC547
D1 to D8	3mm red LEDs (8 off, see text)

Miscellaneous

S1	Push to make, non-locking push button switch
S2	6 way 2 pole rotary (only one pole used)
S3	s.p.s.t. min toggle switch
B1	9 volt (6 x HP7 cells in holder)
SK1	5 way 180 degree DIN socket
X1	2MHz crystal, HC-49/U case
	0.1 inch stripboard 63 holes by 30 strips
	Medium size metal or plastic box
	8 pin DIL i.c. holder
	14 pin DIL i.c. holder
	16 pin DIL i.c. holder
	40 pin DIL i.c. holder
	PP3 type battery connector

5 | THRU box

T he most common method of connecting MIDI units together is the 'chain' system. This has the 'OUT' socket of the master unit connected to the 'IN' socket of the first slave unit. The 'THRU' output of the first slave unit connects to the 'IN' socket of the next slave device in the chain, the THRU output of the second slave unit connects to the 'IN' socket of the third unit, and so on. The signal provided by a 'THRU' output is simply a replica of the signal received at the input. This system therefore couples the signal from one unit to the next, taking the signal from the MIDI master unit to every slave device in the system.

Provided each unit in the system has a 'THRU' socket, it is physically possible to wire any number of units together in this fashion. It is still possible to do this if one slave unit lacks a 'THRU' socket. This device is simply placed at the end of the chain. Provided you are using modern instruments it is unlikely that there will be any problem with a lack of 'THRU' sockets. The same is not true if your system includes several older instruments. In the early days of MIDI it was quite normal for keyboard instruments to lack this facility, and it does not seem to be an absolute requirement of the MIDI specification that such a socket should be fitted.

Although it is physically possible to connect any number of units together using the chain system, this is not guaranteed to provide satisfactory results. Each time the signal is passed from an 'IN' socket to a 'THRU' type it becomes slightly degraded. The cumulative effect

THRU box board layout

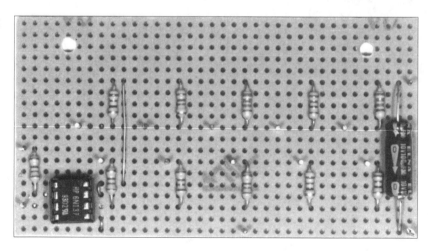

of feeding a signal down a long chain of devices can be a significant distortion of the waveform, or 'smearing' as it is termed. This is not just of academic importance, since the timing of a serial signal such as a MIDI type is crucial. Very small changes in the relative timing of the signal can result in the serial to parallel conversion circuit producing the wrong eight bit binary codes. This can lead to problems with notes being left switched on, incorrect notes being played, etc.

In practice it is unlikely that anyone would ever string together so many MIDI devices that this so-called 'MIDI delay' problem would ever arise. However, any risk of this problem can be avoided using the 'star' method of connection. This requires a MIDI controller which has multiple outputs, and a separate MIDI 'OUT' socket is then used for each 'IN' socket on the slave devices. This version of the star system is not normally a practical proposition, since few MIDI controllers have enough outputs. In fact most only have a single output.

The way around this problem is to use a MIDI THRU box. This is a device which has an input socket, plus what is typically about half a dozen 'THRU' sockets. The output of the MIDI controller is coupled to the 'IN' socket of the THRU box. The slave devices have their inputs driven from the 'THRU' sockets. Obviously the THRU box must have at least one 'THRU' socket per slave unit.

Although the star method of connection is not really necessary in most cases, some MIDI users seem to prefer this system. For users of large MIDI systems I suppose it does have some 'peace of mind' value. If two or more of the slave units lack 'THRU' sockets, then the star system is the only way of connecting everything together properly. The THRU box featured here has five outputs, but this can easily be extended to as many as ten outputs.

Circuit operation

The full circuit diagram for the THRU box appears in Figure 5.1. The unit is based on a high quality opto-isolator (IC1). This has the usual infra-red LED on the input side, plus discrete current limiting resistor R1. On the output side of the device there is a photodiode, an amplifier, a logic gate, and an open-collector output transistor. It is a very fast device by opto-isolator standards. In fact it is so fast that there is no detectable smearing of the signal after passing through this device. The built-in logic gate enables the device to be held in the off state by taking pin 7 low. This facility is not required in the present application, so the device is held in the active state by connecting pin 7 to the positive supply rail.

The open collector output stage of IC1 is ideal for driving the

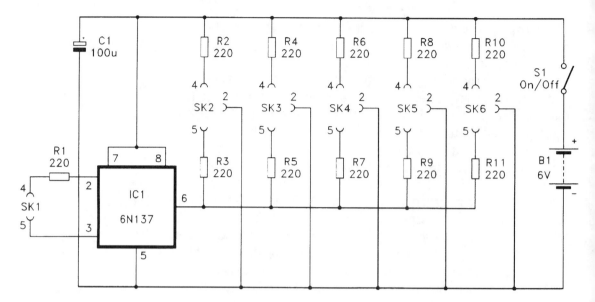

Figure 5.1 The MIDI THRU box circuit diagram

'THRU' outputs. The five output sockets are each driven via a pair of current limiting resistors. It seems to be standard practice for MIDI outputs to have this twin resistor arrangement, and things are presumably done this way as a safety measure to ensure that fault conditions will not result in damage to the opto-isolators at MIDI inputs. The 6N137 opto-isolator can provide output currents of up to about 50 milliamps, and about 5 milliamps flows though each output. Up to ten outputs can therefore be driven, and it is just a matter of adding a pair of resistors and a socket for each additional output that is required. The circuit is powered from a 6 volt battery, and the quiescent current consumption is about 10 milliamps.

Construction

The stripboard component layout is shown in Figure 5.2, and the underside view of the board appears in Figure 5.3. The board has 36 holes by 19 copper strips. Details of the wiring to S1 and the six sockets are provided in Figure 5.4 (which should be used in conjunction with Figure 5.2). Construction of the component panel is very straightforward. The 6N137 is not a static-sensitive device incidentally, but it may well be supplied in some form of anti-static packing. The component layout is easily extended to accommodate more outputs, but the board will need to be six holes wider per additional output.

As will be apparent from Figures 5.1 and 5.4, pin 2 on each output socket is connected to the earth rail of the THRU box. Pin 2 connects to the screen of the MIDI cable, which is needed to prevent the

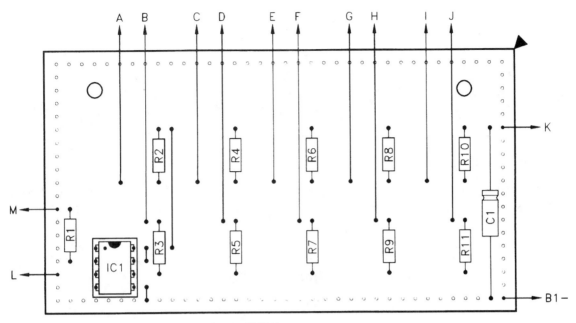

Figure 5.2 The stripboard layout for the THRU box

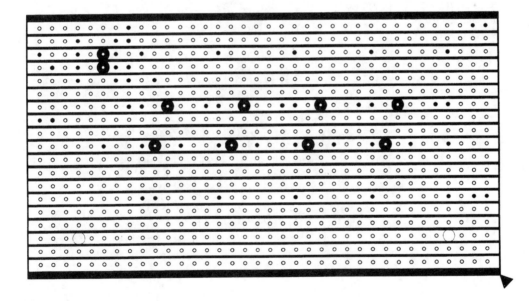

connecting cables from radiating radio frequency interference. Chassis mounting 5 way DIN sockets normally have a large tag opposite pin 2. This simply connects to the metal casing of the socket. As shown in Figure 5.4, the chassis tag and pin 2 of each output socket are wired together. Note that the chassis tag and pin 2 of input socket SK1 are left unconnected. No earth connections are included on MIDI inputs as they would bypass the opto-isolation, and encourage 'hum' loops, etc.

Figure 5.3 The underside of the THRU box stripboard. The board has 36 holes by 19 strips

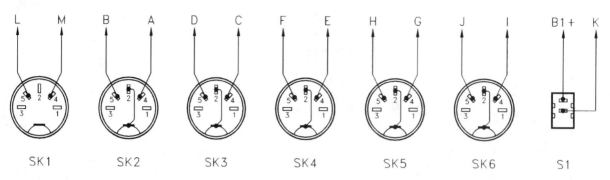

Figure 5.4 The point-to-point wiring for the THRU box

The battery pack consists of four HP7 size cells fitted in a plastic holder. The connections to the holder are made via an ordinary PP3 type battery clip.

Components (THRU box)

Resistors (all 0.25 watt 5% carbon film.

R1 to R11   220R (11 off)

Capacitor

C1   100u 10V axial elect

Semiconductor

IC1   6N137 opto-isolator

Miscellaneous

SK1 to SK6   5 way 180 degree DIN socket (6 off)
S1   s.p.s.t. min toggle
B1   6 volt (4 x HP7 cells in holder)
                     Medium size metal or plastic case
                     Stripboard 36 holes by 19 strips
                     PP3 size battery connector
                     8 pin DIL i.c. holder

MIDI auto switcher

A MIDI system normally has one controller, which in most cases is either a computer running sequencer software, or a keyboard. A real-time sequencing system has what, on the face of it, is two controllers. These are the sequencer, and the keyboard that is used to play tracks into the sequencer. Strictly speaking though, this is two MIDI systems, with each one having its own controller. When recording sequences the keyboard is the controller, and the sequencer is the slave. When playing back sequences the sequencer is the controller, and the instruments are the slave units. There can only be two controllers functioning simultaneously if a MIDI merge unit is used to combine the outputs of the two units into a single data stream, effectively giving a single controller.

MIDI merge units are very useful devices, but are extremely complex. In fact they are normally based on microprocessors, as a fair amount of processing is needed in order to merge the data streams in a way that does not result in data from one MIDI message being mixed into another message by mistake. A unit of this type certainly goes well beyond the scope of this book. However, for many applications some form of switching unit is all that is needed.

A unit of this type enables two or more controllers to drive the slave devices, but not simultaneously. For example, suppose that you have a sequencing system, and that you have more than one keyboard, or perhaps a keyboard and some other form of controller (a MIDI guitar, pedal unit, or whatever). If you wish to keep swapping between one controller and another, a lot of plugging-in and unplugging will be required. Apart from the inconvenience, this is undesirable as it could eventually result in the plugs and sockets wearing out prematurely.

A MIDI switching unit has two or more inputs and a single output.

MIDI auto switcher

In use, the various MIDI controllers that you will wish to use are connected to the inputs, and the output socket connects to the slave units. With a basic manual switching unit a rotary switch is used to select which input is coupled through to the output. Switching from one controller to another is just a matter of resetting the rotary switch to the correct position. Manual MIDI switchers will be covered in the next chapter of this book.

For most purposes a unit that provides automatic switching is more convenient. There is no need to set a switch to select a particular controller, you simply start using that controller, and its output signal is fed through to the slave units. There is a drawback to this system in that most automatic MIDI switching units do not actually provide a switching action. Instead, all the inputs are permanently fed through to the output socket. In use the unit seems to provide a switching action, but it is not.

The practical importance of this is that a malfunction is almost certain to occur if two or more sources are used simultaneously. The input signals will simply be mixed together to form a muddle of signals which will be largely meaningless to the slave units. In many cases this will not be a major problem since there will be little risk of two or more control units operating simultaneously. Also, if a controller should be accidentally activated at the wrong time, there may be little risk of it producing serious consequences. However, in certain circumstances a manual switching unit is a better choice. In particular, for 'live' performances an automatic switcher could produce dire consequences if someone should happen to lean on a keyboard at the wrong time! Use of a manual switcher eliminates this possibility.

Circuit operation

The circuit diagram for the MIDI auto switcher appears in Figure 6.1. As described here the unit has four inputs, but it is easily modified to have any desired number of inputs. Each input socket is coupled to a 6N139 opto isolator. The outputs of these are simply wired together, and drive output socket SK5 via current limiting resistors R9 and R10.

Normally it is not acceptable to wire outputs together in this fashion, but the 6N139 has open collector outputs. This makes it impossible for one output to drive a high current through another output. Having two outputs active at once has much the same effect as having just one output switched on. In both cases a current of about 5 milliamps flows through the output circuit. It is this factor that causes the input signals to be jumbled together at the output if more than

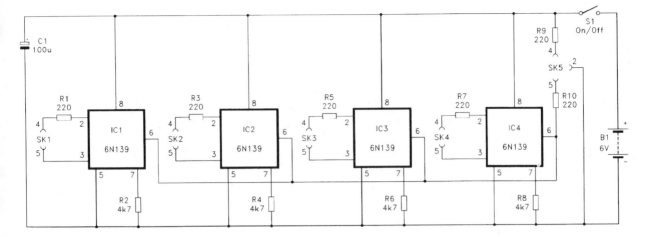

one input signal at a time is received.

If less than four inputs are needed, one or two stages can be omitted. For example, if only two inputs are required, IC1, IC2, R1 to R4, SK1, and SK2 would be omitted. If more inputs are needed, then extra stages can be added. Each stage consists of a 6N139, an input socket plus 220R series resistor, and a 4k7 load resistor. Pin 6 of every 6N139 connects to R10. You can have as many extra stages as you wish and, in theory at any rate, the circuit should work perfectly well with several hundred inputs.

The standby current consumption of the circuit is very low, and could well be no more than a few microamps. With a continuous stream of MIDI messages being passed by the unit the current consumption is still only about 2 milliamps. The 6 volt battery pack should therefore last many months even if the unit receives a great deal of use.

Construction

Details of the MIDI auto switcher component board are provided in Figures 6.2 (component side) and 6.3 (copper side). The point-to-point wiring is illustrated in Figure 6.4. The board has 52 holes by 17 copper strips. The layout has been designed to make it easy to add more stages. The board must be 12 holes wider per additional stage. It only requires a modicum of common sense in order to work out how to fit the extra stages into the layout, but do not forget the seven extra breaks in the copper strips for each additional stage.

The battery consists of four HP7 size cells in a plastic holder. The connections to the holder are made via a PP3 style battery connector.

Figure 6.1 The MIDI auto switcher circuit diagram. Only one input at a time should be used

User tips

The system is wired-up using normal 5 way DIN MIDI cables. Simply connect the output of each controller to an input of the switcher. The output of the switcher connects to the slave devices using whatever method of connection you normally utilize. Try each controller in turn to check that its output signal couples through to the slave units correctly. If one of the inputs does not operate properly, the most likely cause is that the two leads to its DIN socket are connected the wrong way round. If not, check for short circuits on the underside of the component panel in the area occupied by the non-functioning stage.

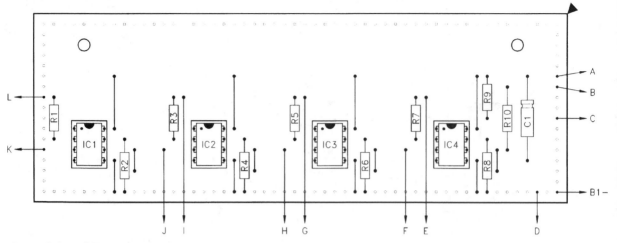

Figure 6.2 The MIDI auto switcher component layout. The board has 52 holes by 17 copper strips

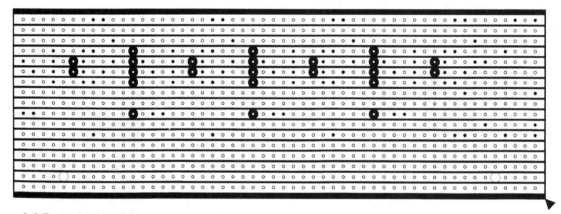

Figure 6.3 The underside of the MIDI auto switcher board

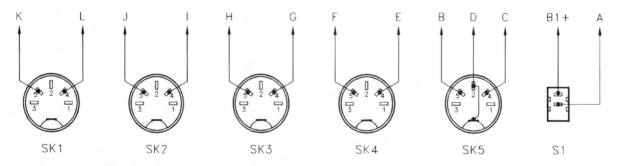

Figure 6.4 The point-to-point wiring for the MIDI auto switcher

Components (MIDI auto switcher)

Resistors (all 0.25 watt 5% carbon film)

R1	220R
R2	4k7
R3	220R
R4	4k7
R5	220R
R6	4k7
R7	220R
R8	4k7
R9	220R
R10	220R

Capacitor

C1	100u 10V axial elect

Semiconductors

IC1 to IC4	6N139 opto-isolator (4 off)

Miscellaneous

SK1 to SK5	5 way 180 degree DIN sockets (5 off)
S1	s.p.s.t. min toggle switch
B1	6 volt (4 x HP7 size cells in plastic holder)
	Stripboard 52 holes by 17 strips
	Medium size metal or plastic case
	Battery clip (PP3 type)
	8 pin DIL i.c. holder (4 off)

7

Auto/manual switcher

A s pointed out previously, there is a potential problem with the auto MIDI switcher unit in that it is possible to accidentally scramble together the signals from two or more sources. In some situations it is better to have a unit that will only allow one signal source to drive the input. Any input signals which are accidentally fed to the unit will then be blocked, and will not produce embarrassing results during 'live' performances.

The circuit of Figure 7.1 is for a MIDI switcher that attempts to provide the 'best of both worlds' by offering both manual and automatic operation. The circuit is basically the same as that for the auto switcher, but an on/off switch has been added in series with each input socket. If a switch is closed, the relevant input is active and can drive the output. If a switch is open, its input is turned off. If the unit is used with just one switch closed, it effectively becomes a manual switching unit, and only one input will be active. At the other extreme the unit can be used with all four switches closed so that it provides fully automatic operation. It can also be used between the two extremes. For example, suppose that you will only be using two of four available controllers in the immediate future. Two switches would be closed in order to make the two required inputs active. The other two switches would be opened so that accidental input signals to the other two inputs would be blocked.

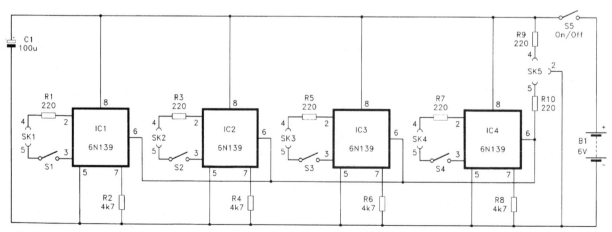

Figure 7.1 The circuit diagram for the auto/manual switcher

Construction

The circuit board is exactly the same as the one for the MIDI auto switcher. The hard wiring is different though, due to the addition of the four switches. Figure 7.2 shows the point-to-point wiring for the auto/manual switching unit. To test the finished unit have S1 to S4 closed, and then make sure that a signal applied to each input is coupled through to the slave units connected to the output socket.

Figure 7.2 The auto/manual switcher hard wiring

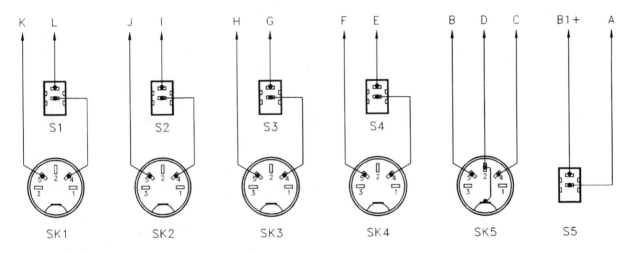

Components (Auto/manual switcher)

Resistors (all 0.25 watt 5% carbon film)

R1	220R
R2	4k7
R3	220R
R4	4k7
R5	220R
R6	4k7
R7	220R
R8	4k7
R9	220R
R10	220R

Capacitor

C1	100u 10V axial elect

Semiconductors

IC1 to IC4	6N139 opto-isolator (4 off)

Miscellaneous

SK1 to SK5	5 way 180 degree DIN sockets (5 off)
S1 to S5	s.p.s.t. min toggle switch (5 off)
B1	6 volt (4 x HP7 size cells in plastic holder)
	Stripboard 52 holes by 17 strips
	Medium size metal or plastic case
	Battery clip (PP3 type)
	8 pin DIL i.c. holder (4 off)

Manual switcher

A manual switching unit is very simple indeed, and is a purely passive device. It really just consists of the input and output sockets, a multi-way switch, and a lot of wiring. Figure 8.1 shows the circuit diagram for a four way manual switching unit.

SK1 is the output socket, and SK2 to SK5 are the input sockets. As a point of interest, the unit will work perfectly well with SK1 as an input, and SK2 to SK5 as outputs, but the unit is of less practical value when used this way round. S1 is a three pole switch which connects pins 2, 4, and 5 of SK1 through to the same pins of whichever input socket is selected.

On the face of it, this circuit is not strictly in accordance with the standard MIDI method, which would have pin 2 of each input socket left unconnected. However, in this case it would not be a good idea to leave pin 2 unconnected, as this would leave the screen of the output cable 'floating'. It is better if pin 2 is coupled through to pin 2 of the output socket. The screen of the output lead is then earthed at the MIDI controller, and there should be no problems with the cables

Figure 8.1 The manual switcher circuit diagram

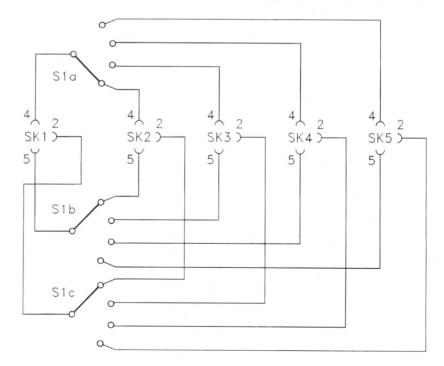

radiating radio frequency interference. The units wired to the input sockets do not have all their earths wired together via this unit, since S1c ensures that only one input at a time has its earth connection coupled to anything. Consequently, there is no way that this device can introduce 'hum' loops, or other earthing related problems.

Construction

Construction of this project is just a matter of mounting S1 and all the switches on the front panel of the case and then wiring-up every-thing correctly. This wiring is shown in Figure 8.2. For the sake of clarity, the wiring is shown in three stages (one wiring diagram for each pole of S1). The wiring should be quite easy provided all the tags of S1 and pins 2, 4, and 5 of every socket are well 'tinned' with solder before any wires are added. Once the tinning has been com-

Figure 8.2 The manual switcher hard wiring

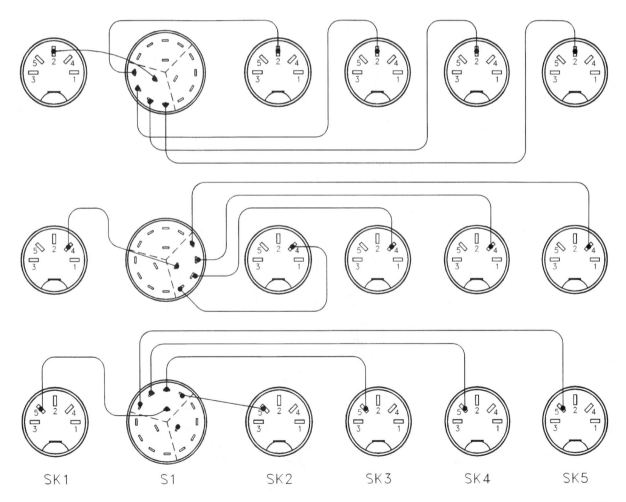

SK1   S1   SK2   SK3   SK4   SK5

pleted, work through the wiring methodically, which will reduce the risk of missed out or crossed-over wires. It is difficult to make this kind of wiring really neat, but at least try to keep the wiring to each pole of S1 reasonably well separated. This will make life much easier if a mistake is made, and the wiring has to be searched for the error.

Checking the finished unit is very straightforward. Connect a MIDI source to each input, and a slave unit to the output. Then check that at each setting of S1 the appropriate controller is coupled through to the slave unit.

Components

Miscellaneous

S1	4 way 3 pole rotary
SK1 to SK5	5 way 180 degree DIN sockets (5 off)
	Control knob

A MIDI patch-bay is really a form of THRU box, albeit a rather elaborate one. A MIDI patch-bay has a number of MIDI inputs and outputs. The basic idea is to have the output of each MIDI controller coupled to an input of the patch-bay. Similarly, the MIDI input socket of each slave device is connected to an output of the patch-bay. A bank of switches control which output (if any) is driven from each input. Each output can be driven from any input, or several inputs if required. A MIDI patch-bay is more than a little useful if you need to frequently reconfigure your system. There is no need to keep unplugging and plugging-in MIDI leads. Instead you just flick a few switches in order to reconfigure the system.

The patch-bay featured here has three inputs and four outputs. This imbalance in the numbers of inputs and outputs is deliberate, and is included because most MIDI systems have more slave units than devices which will at some time be used as the controller. Although the unit has just three inputs and four outputs, it is not difficult to extend the circuit to have up to about 12 inputs and outputs.

It is important to realise that this patch-bay, unlike the sophisticated ready-made variety, does not have a built-in merge facility. Like the automatic switcher unit described previously, this patch-bay must

MIDI patch-bay

only be supplied with one input signal at a time. Feeding it with more than one input signal at a time will result in the two signals being scrambled together, giving an output signal that the slave units will not be able to decode correctly.

Circuit operation

The full circuit diagram for the MIDI patch-bay appears in Figure 9.1. SK1, SK2, and SK3 are the input sockets, while SK4 to SK7 are the four output sockets.

If we ignore IC2 and IC3 for the moment, and S1, S4, S7 and S10 are closed, the circuit acts as a straightforward THRU box having four outputs. However, due to the inclusion of the switches, any output can be deactivated by opening the relevant switch. For example, SK5 can be switched off by opening S4. With IC2 and IC3 taken into account, the circuit is very much like the automatic switcher unit described previously. The output of each opto-isolator drives the output sockets via its own set of four switches though, so that each input can be coupled through any given output, or not, depending on the setting of the relevant switch. The circuit is basically a combination of a THRU box and an automatic switcher, with switches to control exactly what is coupled to where.

Figure 9.1 The MIDI patch-bay circuit diagram. There are three inputs and four outputs

If required, more outputs can be added. For each additional out-

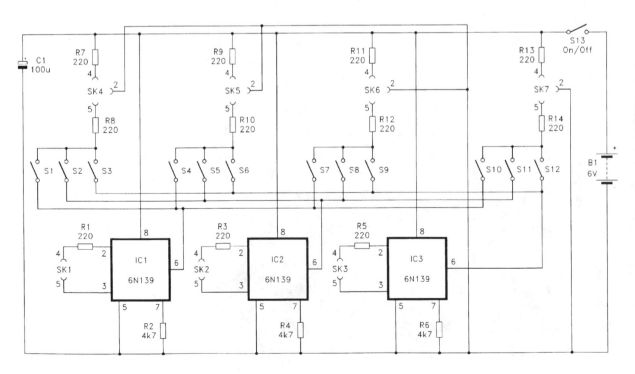

put an extra output socket will be needed, together with two series resistors and a set of three switches. Each additional output circuit is connected in exactly the same manner as SK4, R7, R8, S1, S2 and S3. More inputs can be accommodated, and for each one an extra 6N139 opto-isolator will be needed, together with a 220R input resistor and 4k7 load resistor. Also, where banks of three switches are used at present (e.g. S4, S5 and S6), an extra switch will be needed for each additional input.

Construction

Details of the stripboard component panel are shown in Figure 9.2 (component side) and Figure 9.3 (copper side). The board has 35 holes by 23 copper strips, and construction of the circuit board is perfectly straightforward. The hard wiring is somewhat less simple due to the large number of connections involved. This wiring is shown in Figure 9.4. Add the links between SK4 to SK7 first, followed by the connections between each row of switches. Next add the links between the columns of switches. Finally add the connections from the component board to the off-board components. Work through all this wiring in a methodical manner, as this will greatly reduce the risk of an omitted or incorrect connection.

User tips

Testing the unit simply involves checking that the unit provides the correct couplings from the inputs to the outputs. It is probably best to start with all the switches closed, and then check that each input couples through to every output. If the unit provides a full set of couplings it is unlikely that it is faulty, but it would be as well to check that each interconnection can be cut by opening the correct switch.

When using a device of this type for the first time it can get a bit confusing. Life is much easier if you remember that each row of switches is paired with an input. Similarly, each column of switches is paired with an output. In order to couple a given input to a certain output, it is just a matter of selecting the switch which is in the appropriate column and row. For instance, suppose that a coupling is needed between input SK2 and output SK7. SK2 drives the middle row of switches (S2, S5, S7, and S11), while SK7 is driven via the right hand column of switches (S10, S11, and S12). Clearly S11 is the switch that is common to the appropriate row and column, and this switch should be closed, in order to provide a coupling between SK2 and SK7. Table 4 should help to make it easy to find the right switches for any required set of interconnections.

Figure 9.2 The MIDI patch-bay stripboard. This has 35 holes by 23 copper strips

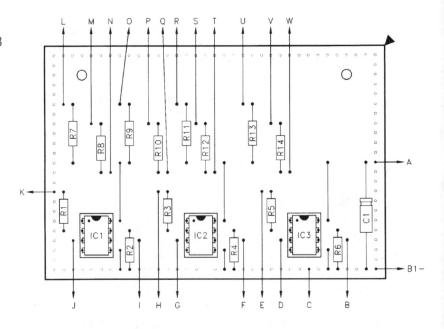

Figure 9.3 The underside of the MIDI patch-bay board

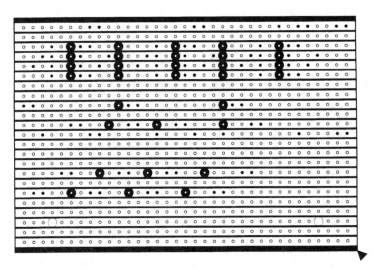

Table 4

	SK4	SK5	SK6	SK7
SK1	S1	S4	S7	S10
SK2	S2	S5	S8	S11
SK3	S3	S6	S9	S12

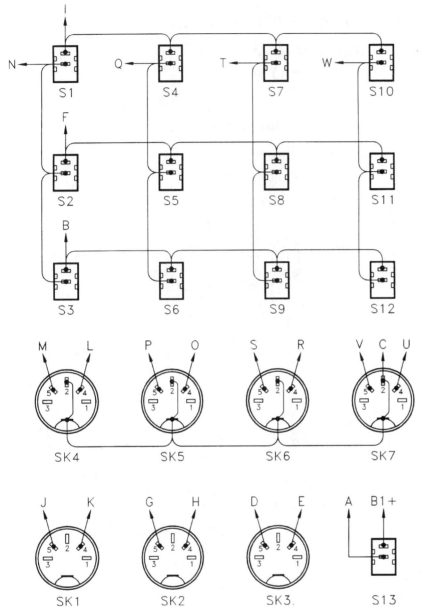

Figure 9.4 Details of the MIDI
patch-bay wiring

Components (MIDI patch-bay)

Resistors (all 0.25 watt 5% carbon film)
R1 to R14   220R (14 off)

Capacitor
C1   100u 10V axial elect

Semiconductors
IC1 to IC3   6N139 opto-isolator (3 off)

Miscellaneous

S1 to S13   s.p.s.t min toggle (13 off)
SK1 to SK7   5 way 180 degree DIN socket (7 off)
B1   6 volt (4 x HP7 size cells in plastic holder)
                Large plastic or aluminium case
                Stripboard 35 holes by 23 strips
                Battery connector (PP3 type)
                8 pin DIL i.c. holder (3 off)

MIDI controlled switcher 10

With complex MIDI systems there are often more available voices than there are MIDI channels to accommodate them. Sixteen channels seemed reasonably generous when MIDI was first devised, but advances in electronic musical instruments soon made the provision of sixteen channels seem inadequate. Some instruments can occupy all sixteen channels on their own, and a fair percentage of modern instruments can occupy eight or more channels.

Ideally the controller should have several independent MIDI outputs, effectively giving dozens of MIDI channels. This is a feature which is still relatively rare though, and most users have to do the best they can with a single MIDI output. One way of stretching the scope of a single MIDI output is to use some form of MIDI controlled switching unit so that instruments can be selected and deselected in mid-sequence. Most users do not need to use dozens of voices simultaneously, but instead just need some means of selecting the required voices 'on the fly'.

This project is a more advanced version of a THRU box. It has one input and four THRU outputs, and it is connected into the MIDI system in exactly the same manner as a conventional THRU box. However, it is much more sophisticated than a normal THRU box, as it will respond to program change messages from the controller. It is preset to operate on MIDI channel 1, but can be wired to operate on any desired MIDI channel. It responds to MIDI program numbers from 0 to 15. The program change number controls which outputs are active, and which are switched off. Any required on/off combination can be obtained by using the appropriate control change number.

The MIDI controlled switcher

71

One simple way of using the unit would be to have two instruments operating on channels 1 to 8, and two instruments operating on channels 9 to 16. At any one time, only one of the units on channels 1 to 8 would be active. Similarly, only one of the units on channels 9 to 16 would be active at one time. Program change messages would be used to switch from one unit to the other, as required.

Of course, three or four instruments could be simultaneously active if required, perhaps in order to build up some complex layered sounds. Practical setups will often be rather less straightforward than the one outlined above, and it might be necessary to have two or more 'chained' instruments connected to some outputs. Some careful thought and planning will usually be needed in order to get the most from any complex MIDI system, including one which incorporates this unit.

Circuit operation

Refer to Figure 10.1 for the MIDI controlled switcher circuit diagram. The part of the circuit around IC2 forms what is basically just a simple MIDI THRU box. SK1 is the input socket, and SK2 to SK5 are the four THRU output sockets. Matters are only complicated by the inclusion of a switching transistor in series with each output socket (TR2 to TR5). Each transistor has a base resistor which gives compatibility with normal logic circuit levels. A high input level switches off the transistor (and its corresponding output). A low input level switches on the transistor, and activates the output socket that it is driving. IC6 is a quad 'D' type flip/flop, and it provides the four control signals for the electronic switches.

A MIDI program change message is a simple two byte type. The first byte contains the program change message code, and the channel number. The second byte contains the program number, and it is the lower nibble of this byte that must be latched onto the outputs of IC6. TR1, IC1, and IC3 are a clock generator and UART that provides the serial to parallel conversion. IC4 is an 8 bit comparator, and in this case its function is to compare the bit patterns from the UART with the bit pattern hard wired onto its eight 'Q' inputs. The upper nibble is wired with the binary pattern 1100, which is the program change message code.

The lower nibble is wired with the binary pattern 0000, which places the unit on MIDI channel 1. If required, a different MIDI channel can be selected by hard wiring the appropriate value onto pins 12, 14, 16, and 18 of IC4. However, remember that the convention is for MIDI channels to be numbered from 1 to 16, whereas the values used

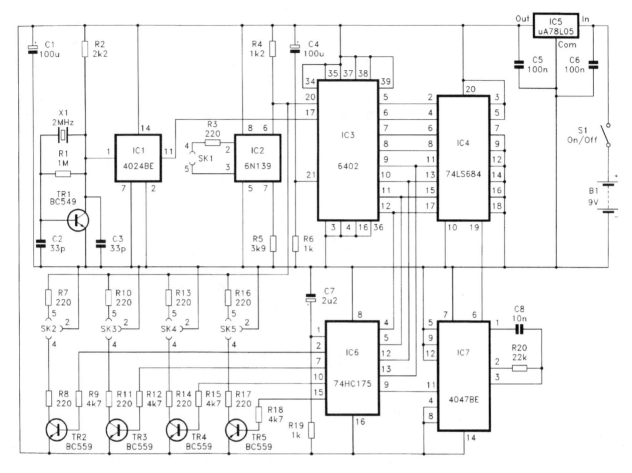

Figure 10.1 The MIDI controlled switcher circuit diagram

in channel messages are from 0 to 15. Hence the binary value fed to IC4 must be one less than the required channel number. Channel 1 will probably be the most convenient one to use, and there is no point in altering the wiring unless it is really necessary to place the unit on another channel.

The output at pin 19 of IC4 goes low when it detects a program change message on the appropriate channel. This is used to trigger IC7, which operates as a monostable having an output pulse duration of just over 0.5ms. It is assumed here that the next byte will be the program number, and that it will follow on almost immediately after the header byte. This results in the output pulse from IC7 ending while the program number is present on the outputs of IC3. This in turn results in the lower four bits of this number being latched into IC6, which has its 'clock pulse' input fed from the output of IC7.

The MIDI standard does not require that header bytes should be immediately followed by any data bytes that are needed to complete the message. In practice though, this is the most convenient way of doing things, and any gap would be undesirable as it would encourage

MIDI 'choke'. On trying out the prototype MIDI controlled switcher with a variety of master units, it worked with perfect reliability in every case.

There is another potential cause of problems in that the MIDI standard does allow MIDI timing signals to be sent in the middle of other messages. In theory at any rate, it would be possible to have a program change header byte followed by a MIDI clock message. This would clearly cause a malfunction of the unit. In reality it seems to be very unusual for timing signals to be sent within other messages, and there is little likelihood of this factor causing problems. It is something the user should be aware of though, and the unit should not be used with a master unit that produces timing messages that could cause malfunctions.

A 5 volt regulated supply is obtained from a 9 volt battery via a monolithic voltage regulator. The current consumption of the circuit is quite high at about 40 milliamps or so. The majority of the supply current is drawn by IC4. A 74LS device has to be used here, since no high speed CMOS version (which would have a vastly lower current consumption) seems to be available. The battery must be a fairly high capacity type, such as six HP7 size cells in a holder.

Construction

Details of the stripboard panel are provided in Figures 10.2 and 10.3, while Figure 10.4 shows the hard wiring. The board has 72 holes by 39 copper strips. This can conveniently be a piece cut from a standard size board having 117 holes by 39 strips. Construction of the board is not particularly difficult, but the relatively large size and complexity of the board is a factor that has to be taken into account. With a substantial number of components and link-wires to be fitted there is plenty of opportunity for mistakes to be made! Rushing at things is not likely to result in a board that works first time. Success is much more likely if you take things steadily and systematically. This project is not really suitable for those who have little or no previous experience of electronic project construction. Remember that IC1, IC3, IC6, and IC7 are all MOS devices that require the usual anti-static handling precautions.

User tips

At switch-on IC6 is provided with a reset pulse that sets all its outputs low, and switches on all four MIDI outputs. Therefore, initially

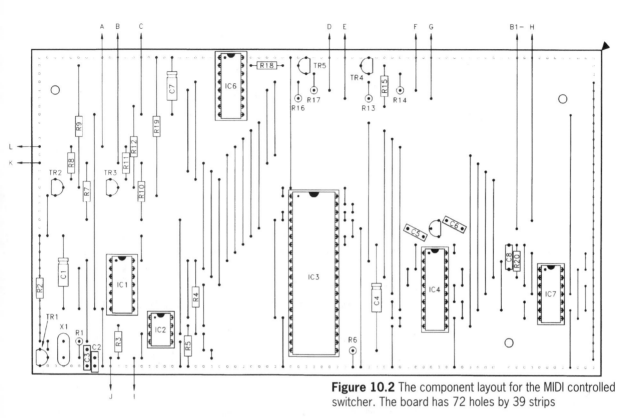

Figure 10.2 The component layout for the MIDI controlled switcher. The board has 72 holes by 39 strips

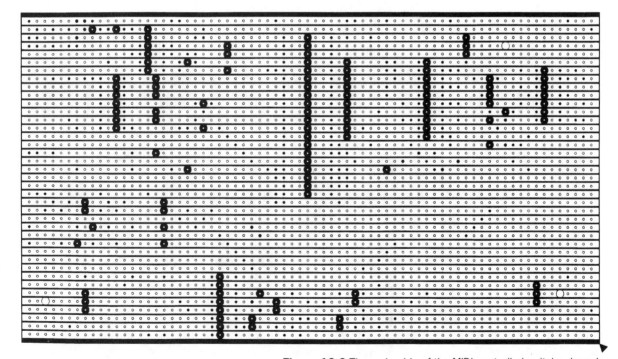

Figure 10.3 The underside of the MIDI controlled switcher board

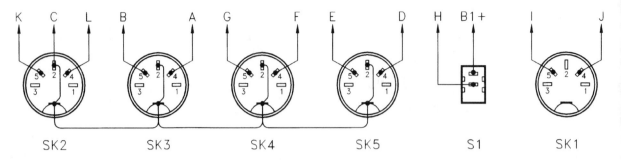

Figure 10.4 The MIDI controlled switcher wiring

the unit should operate as a conventional THRU box, with all four outputs operational. Table 5 shows the set of on/off states produced for program numbers from 0 to 15.

Program change messages are a convenient means of controlling MIDI gadgets since they can be generated quite easily using most MIDI master units. For instance, most MIDI keyboards and keyboard instruments have push-button controls that can be used to generate these messages. There should be no difficulty in recording program change messages into a real-time sequencer, and many sequencers now allow these messages to be added anywhere in a score using the editing facilities. Bear in mind that this unit will not respond instantly to program change messages. The delay in its response is very short, and is actually well under a millisecond. Even so, sending another message immediately after a program change type could result in the header byte of that message being corrupted at one or more of the outputs.

Table 5

Prog change value	SK2	SK3	SK4	SK5
0	ON	ON	ON	ON
1	OFF	ON	ON	ON
2	ON	OFF	ON	ON
3	OFF	OFF	ON	ON
4	ON	ON	OFF	ON
5	OFF	ON	OFF	ON
6	ON	OFF	OFF	ON
7	OFF	OFF	OFF	ON
8	ON	ON	ON	OFF
9	OFF	ON	ON	OFF
10	ON	OFF	ON	OFF
11	OFF	OFF	ON	OFF
12	ON	ON	OFF	OFF
13	OFF	ON	OFF	OFF
14	ON	OFF	OFF	OFF
15	OFF	OFF	OFF	OFF

Note that program change values from 16 to 31 have the same effect as those from 0 to 15, as do values from 32 to 47, 48 to 63, 64 to 79, 80 to 95, 96 to 111, and 112 to 127.

Components (MIDI controlled switcher)

Resistors (all 0.25 watt 5% carbon film)

R1	1M
R2	2k2
R3	220R
R4	1k2
R5	3k9
R6	1k
R7	220R
R8	220R
R9	4k7
R10	220R
R11	220R
R12	4k7
R13	220R
R14	220R
R15	4k7
R16	220R
R17	220R
R18	4k7
R19	1k
R20	22k

Semiconductors

IC1	4024BE
IC2	6N139 opto-isolator
IC3	6402 or AY-3-1015D UART
IC4	74LS684
IC5	uA78L05 (5V 100mA positive regulator)
IC6	74HC175
IC7	4047BE
TR1	BC549
TR2	BC559
TR3	BC559
TR4	BC559
TR5	BC559

Capacitors

C1	100u 10V axial elect
C2	33p ceramic plate
C3	33p ceramic plate
C4	100u 10V axial elect
C5	100n disc ceramic
C6	100n disc ceramic
C7	2u2 63V axial elect
C8	10n polyester

Miscellaneous

SK1 to SK5	5 way 180 degree DIN socket (5 off)
S1	s.p.s.t min toggle switch
X1	2MHz crystal, HC-49/U case
B1	9 volt (6 x HP7 size cells in plastic holder)
	Large metal or plastic case
	Stripboard 72 holes by 39 strips
	8 pin DIL i.c. holder
	14 pin DIL i.c. holder (2 off)
	16 pin DIL i.c. holder
	20 pin DIL i.c. holder
	40 pin DIL i.c. holder
	Battery connector (PP3 type)

11 | MIDI lead tester

P robably the least reliable part of a MIDI system is the connecting leads. This is not really due to a serious lack of quality in the leads, but is more due to the fact that leads tend to get kicked around, tripped over, trodden on, and generally abused. A problem for those who are into building electronic equipment is that they tend to get the job of testing other peoples' MIDI leads as well as their own!

MIDI leads can be checked using a multi-range test meter set to a resistance range, but this tends to be a rather fiddly job due to the smallness and close spacing of the pins on the DIN plugs. Temporarily fitting a DIN socket onto each plug makes matters a bit easier, but if you are going to do a lot of MIDI lead testing it is worthwhile making up a lead tester. The very simple lead tester featured here enables MIDI leads to be quickly and easily checked. The five LED display will show up both broken wires and short circuits between wires.

Circuit operation

The circuit is basically just an oscillator which drives a five LED display via the MIDI lead under test. Figure 11.1 shows the lead tester circuit diagram. The oscillator is a straightforward 555 timer used in the standard astable (oscillator) mode. An ordinary 555 will work in this circuit, but it is advisable to use a low power version in order to keep the current consumption down to a reasonable level. The values of the three timing components (R1, R2, and C2) have been chosen to give a roughly squarewave output signal at a frequency of a few hertz. TR1 is used as a simple inverter stage which gives anti-phase output signals (i.e. when pin 3 of IC1 is high, TR1's collector is low, and vice versa).

The anti-phase outputs of the oscillator circuit are used to drive the five LED display via current limiting resistors (R5 to R9) and the lead under test. The test lead is, of course, plugged into SK1 and SK2. With a fault-free MIDI lead D2, D3, and D4 should flash on and off a few times a second, but D2 and D4 should flash out-of-phase with D3 (e.g. when D2 and D4 are switched on, D3 should be switched off). Faulty leads will give different results. A full explana-

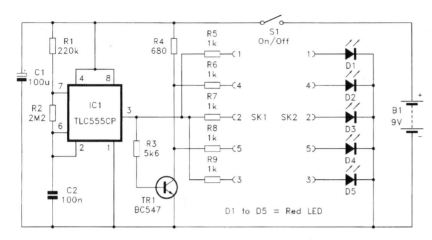

Figure 11.1 The MIDI lead tester circuit. TR1 provides an anti-phase signal

tion of the results produced by various faults are described in detail in the 'User Tips' section on page 81.

The current consumption of the circuit is about 7 milliamps with no LEDs switched on, but is substantially higher than this when one or more LEDs are activated. Despite the relatively high current consumption a small (PP3 size) battery should be adequate as the power source. Presumably the unit will only be used intermittently and for short periods.

Construction

Refer to Figures 11.2 to 11.4 for details of the MIDI lead tester component board and point-to-point wiring. The board has 36 holes by 19 copper strips. Construction of the board presents no real difficulties, but there are a few points to note.

Although the TLC555CP is a CMOS device, it does not require anti-static handling precautions due to its built-in protection circuits. The same is true of the other low power timer devices I have encountered.

D1 to D5 are shown as being mounted on the component panel, but if desired they can be mounted off-board on the front panel and hard wired to the component panel. The disadvantage of this method is that it substantially increases what is already rather a lot of point-to-point wiring for such a simple project. The easier method is to mount the LEDs on the board, leaving them with long leads.

The general layout of the unit is then arranged so that with the board mounted inside the case, the LEDs will fit into suitable holes drilled in the front panel. Some careful planning and measuring is needed in order to get this setup just right, but it is generally a more satisfactory way of handling things. I would recommend the use of multi-coloured ribbon cables to carry the connections from the circuit board to the two sockets. As the LED current is not very high it would be advisable to use ultra-bright LEDs in the display.

Figure 11.2 The MIDI lead tester component layout. The board has 36 holes by 19 strips

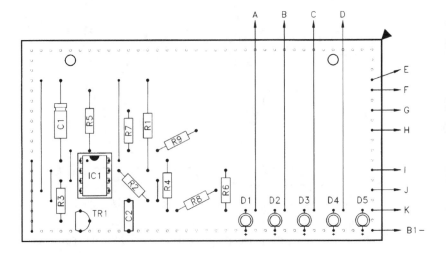

Figure 11.3 The underside of the MIDI lead tester board

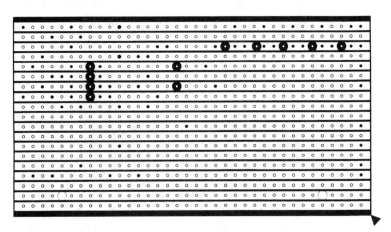

Figure 11.4 The MIDI lead tester wiring

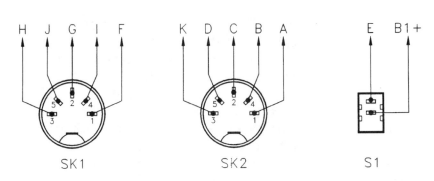

User tips

As pointed out previously, if a functioning lead is connected between SK1 and SK2, D2 and D4 should flash out-of-phase with D3. You will probably find that many MIDI leads cause D1, D3, and D5 to flash out-of-phase with D2 and D4. This is simply because many MIDI leads seem to have pins 1 and 3 on one plug connected through to the same pins on the other plug. Strictly speaking, this is not correct, and these pins should be left unconnected. In practice it is of no real consequence, and a lead having these connections should work perfectly well. Presumably the extra two leads are included in these leads in anticipation of a 'super MIDI' eventually appearing, and requiring these extra connections.

If a LED fails to light up, then there is a break in the cable. For instance, if D4 fails to flash, then the lead carrying the pin 5 to pin 5 connection is clearly broken. Table 6 shows which display LED corresponds to each pin of the connecting cable. Remember that it is perfectly all right if D1 and D5 fail to operate. If a LED flashes erratically or intermittently, this indicates that the corresponding connecting wire of the cable is only making intermittent contact. You may sometimes find that two adjacent LEDs in the display fail to flash, but instead light up at a more or less steady intensity. This indicates that there is a short circuit across the appropriate two connecting leads. The short circuits will almost certainly be at the connections to one or other of the plugs. Provided the plugs are not moulded types, it is not usually too difficult to locate and clear a fault of this type.

Check your leads

One point which must be made is that this tester will not necessarily indicate whether or not a lead is providing the correct connections. In particular, 5 way DIN audio leads often have cross-coupled connections. This method of connection is useless for MIDI use, but could give a normal indication from this tester. If you have problems with a new lead and suspect that it is not providing the right interconnections, it is advisable to thoroughly test it using a continuity tester.

Table 6

LED	Pin no
D1	1
D2	4
D3	2
D4	5
D5	3

Components

Resistors (all 0.25 watt 5% carbon film)

R1	220k
R2	2M2
R3	5k6
R4	680R
R5	1k
R6	1k
R7	1k
R8	1k
R9	1k

Capacitors

C1	100u 10V axial elect
C2	100n polyester

Semiconductors

IC1	TLC555CP, L555CP, or similar
TR1	BC547
D1 to D5	Ultra-bright red LED (5 off)

Miscellaneous

B1	9 volt (PP3 size)
S1	s.p.s.t sub min toggle
SK1,2	5 way 180 degree DIN socket (2 off)
	Stripboard 36 holes by 19 strips
	Small metal or plastic case
	8 pin DIL i.c. holder
	Battery connector

12

Program change pedal

M IDI tends to be regarded as something that is a real boon for musicians who mainly work in a studio, but is of limited value for those who are primarily 'live' performers. While it is probably fair to say that MIDI is of greater importance to studio musicians, it still has great potential for use in 'live' performances.

This device is mainly for use in 'live' performances, and it is a MIDI pedal unit. When the pedal is operated a program change message is generated. This message sets the unit to program 0, although the unit can be wired to use other program numbers if desired.

The main idea of using this unit is to produce a change to a different sound at some point in the proceedings. You start with the instrument set to any program number other than 0, and have the first set of sound generator parameters assigned to that program number. Have the second set of sound generator settings assigned to program number 0. By operating the pedal at the appropriate time a change from the first sound to the second is obtained. Of course, such a change can normally be obtained by operating one or two push-buttons on the instrument, but the pedal allows the 'look no hands' method to be used. This makes it easy to place a seamless program change into the middle of a piece even when performing 'live'. Although this unit is mainly intended for use with a synthesiser or other keyboard instrument, it can obviously be used to control a digital effects unit or any other device which responds to program change messages. If necessary, it can control several units 'chained' together.

Circuit operation

Like some of the other units featured in this book, the program change pedal is based on a UART. However, whereas the other projects have used the receiver section to decode MIDI input signals, in this case it is the transmitter section that is utilized. Figure 12.1 shows the circuit diagram for the MIDI program change pedal. The clock generator circuit is much the same as that used in some of the previous circuits. The 6402 UART has separate receiver and transmitter clock inputs, and in this case it is obviously the transmitter clock

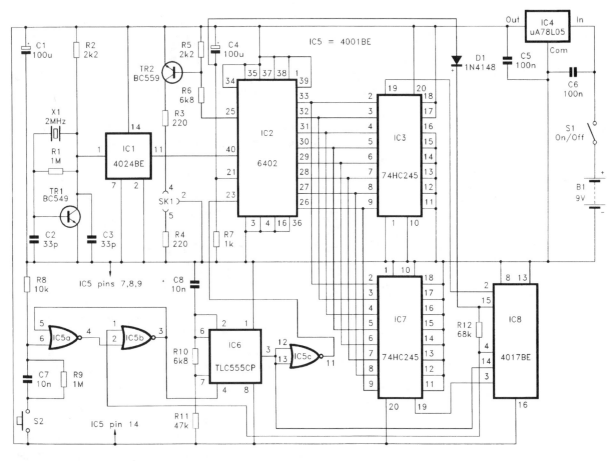

terminal (pin 40) that is fed with the 500kHz output signal from IC1. The control pins of IC2 are wired in exactly the same fashion as in the previous circuits, as these are common to the transmitter and receiver sections.

The serial output signal from pin 25 of IC2 must be converted into a 5 milliamp current loop signal that is compatible with the opto-isolators at MIDI inputs. This is achieved using a simple common emitter switch based on TR2. C4 and R7 provide a positive reset pulse at switch-on.

On the input side of the UART there are two octal tristate buffers (IC3 and IC7). IC3 is the buffer which is active initially, and its inputs are wired with the binary code '11000000'. This is the program change code (1100) plus the channel 1 code (0000). Pins 11 to 14 can be wired with the binary value for a different channel number if desired, but in most cases there will be no practical advantage in doing this. Once IC2 has been activated and has sent the program change header byte, IC3 is switched off and IC7 is switched on. The inputs of IC7 (pins 11 to 18) are wired with the binary code

Figure 12.1 The program change pedal circuit. IC2 is used as a serial transmitter in this circuit

'00000000', and this is the value used in the data byte of the program change message. Again, the inputs could be wired with a different value, but there would normally be no point in doing this. Most instruments permit any set of sound generator settings to be assigned to any program number.

For the circuit to function properly it is necessary for IC3 and IC7 to be fed with the right control signals, and for IC2 to be sent a pulse each time a byte must be transmitted. The control signals for IC3 and IC7 are produced by IC8 which is a one-of-ten decoder. In this case though, the device resets itself via R12 when output '2' goes high, and it really just acts as a form of flip/flop. Outputs '0' and '1' provide the control signals to the tristate buffers. Initially it is IC3 that is active.

IC6 is a 555 timer which operates here as a gated astable (oscillator). It provides the clock signal to IC8, and via an inverter (IC5a) it provides the pulses to activate IC2. If IC6 was simply allowed to free-run, the circuit would repeatedly send program change messages. On the first clock half cycle IC2 would be activated, and would send the header byte. On the next half cycle IC3 would turn off and IC7 would turn on. The third half cycle would activate IC2, and the data byte would be sent. On the fourth half cycle the circuit would be returned to its original state, and on the fifth cycle the whole process would start again from the beginning.

IC6 must be controlled in such a way that on operating the pedal switch this chain of events is started, but once the second byte has be transmitted the process must be brought to a halt. IC6 is controlled by a simple set/reset flip/flop based on two gates of IC5. Normally this flip/flop holds pin 4 of IC6 low so that oscillation is suppressed. S2 is the footswitch, and activating this triggers the flip/flop to the opposite state. IC6 then oscillates, and takes the circuit through the steps described previously. When both bytes of the program change message have been sent, IC8 resets itself and also resets the flip/flop based on IC5. This halts the circuit which has returned to its original set of logic levels. It is therefore ready to send another message when S2 is operated again.

The circuit requires a reasonably stable 5 volt supply. This is derived from a 9 volt battery via a simple regulator circuit based on IC4. The current consumption of the circuit is only about 5 to 6 milliamps, and a PP3 size battery is therefore adequate as the power source. On the other hand, if the unit is likely to be used for long periods of time it would probably be more economic to use a higher capacity battery such as a PP9, or six HP7 cells in a plastic holder.

Construction

Figures 12.2 and 12.3 show the component layout and underside of the program change pedal stripboard. Details of the hard wiring are provided in Figure 12.4. Construction of the board is not particularly difficult, but this is another relatively complex project which is not really suitable for beginners. With the exceptions of IC4 and IC6, the integrated circuits are CMOS types which require the normal anti-static handling precautions. Be careful not to overlook any of the many link wires, or the equally numerous breaks in the copper strips.

S2 can be a heavy duty push-button switch mounted on the top panel of the case. It should be a non-locking (push to make, release to break) type. It might be difficult to obtain a heavy-duty push-button switch of this type, but a large push-button switch of good quality will suffice and should have a reasonably long operating life. A strong case is required for any pedal style project, and a diecast aluminium box is ideal. However, in practice a inexpensive case of folded aluminium construction usually proves to be perfectly adequate, and is a much less expensive option. Most plastic cases are not tough enough for a project such as this.

An alternative approach is to have the footswitch separate from the main unit. Suitable footswitch units are available, and are apparently intended for use with cassette recorders. They are well suited to the present application though. These foot-switches are normally supplied complete with a lead about 1.5 metres long which is terminated with a 2.5 millimetre jack plug. If the unit is used with a footswitch of this type a 2.5 millimetre jack socket must be fitted to the main unit, and connected in place of S2.

User tips

Testing the unit is very straightforward. Couple the output socket to the MIDI 'IN' socket of a synthesiser or other unit that will respond to program change messages. Make sure that the MIDI device is set up to receive MIDI messages on channel 1, and that it is set to a program number other than program 0. Operate S2 and check that the MIDI unit has changed to program 0. Remember that the manufacturer might not use program numbers from 0 to 127. Many seem to use numbers from 1 to 128, or some totally different method such as an alpha-numeric type (e.g. A-1 to H-16). The equipment manuals should clarify the relationship between the true program values and the manufacturer's numbering system.

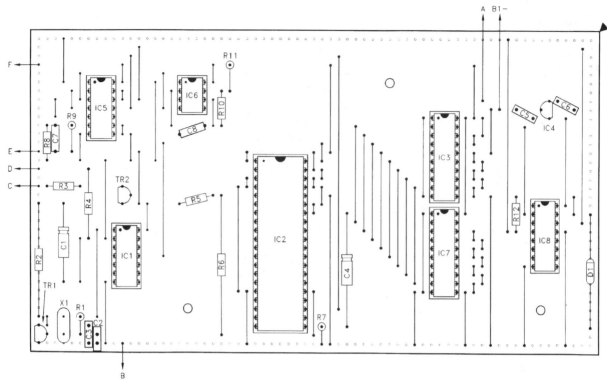

Figure 12.2 The program change pedal component layout. The board has 67 holes by 36 strips

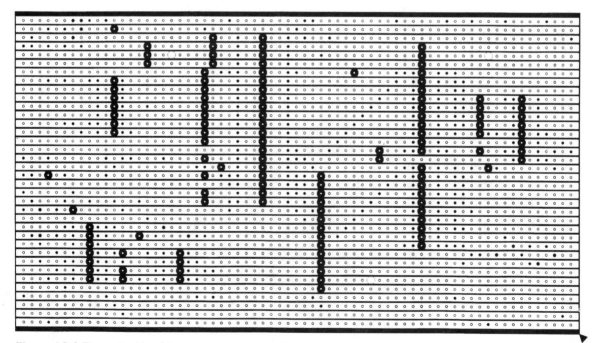

Figure 12.3 The underside of the program change pedal board

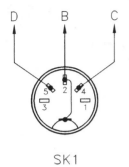
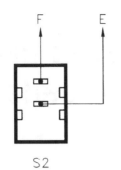
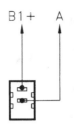

SK1   S2   S1

Figure 12.4 The program change pedal wiring

Components

Resistors (all 0.25 watt 5% carbon film)

R1	1M
R2	2k2
R3	220R
R4	220R
R5	2k2
R6	6k8
R7	1k
R8	10k
R9	1M
R10	6k8
R11	47k
R12	68k

Capacitors

C1	100u 10V axial elect
C2	33p ceramic plate
C3	33p ceramic plate
C4	100u 10V axial elect
C5	100n disc ceramic
C6	100n disc ceramic
C7	10n polyester
C8	10n polyester

Semiconductors

IC1	4024BE
IC2	6402 UART (or equivalent)
IC3	74HC245
IC4	uA78L05 (5V 100mA positive regulator)
IC5	4001BE
IC6	TLC555CP (or equivalent)
IC7	74HC245
IC8	4017BE
TR1	BC549
TR2	BC559
D1	1N4148

Miscellaneous

B1	9 volt (PP3 size)
SK1	5 pin 180 degree DIN socket
S1	s.p.s.t. min toggle switch
S2	heavy duty non-locking push button switch (see text)
X1	2MHz HC-49/U crystal
	Stripboard 67 holes by 36 strips
	battery connector
	8 pin d.i.l. i.c. holder
	14 pin d.i.l. i.c. holder (2 off)
	16 pin d.i.l. i.c. holder
	20 pin d.i.l. i.c. holder (2 off)
	40 pin d.i.l. i.c. holder
	Medium size metal case

Improved program change pedal

13

T his project is basically the same as the one featured previously, but it has a small additional circuit which makes it much more versatile. Like the previous program change pedal, this one produces a change to program number zero when the pedal is first operated. However, whereas the previous circuit always produced messages having a data byte value of zero, this unit increments the program number by one on each operation of the pedal. In other words, the program number is set to zero the first time the pedal is operated, to one the second time it is operated, to two the third time, and so on. This continues until the program number reaches 127. On the subsequent operation of the pedal the program number is cycled back to zero, although it is unlikely that the program number would ever be incremented this far in practice.

This pedal is used in much the same way as the original unit, but you are not limited to having a single change in sound. By setting up the MIDI instrument with the correct sound generator parameters assigned to each program number, you can have dozens of these sound changes. Most instruments make it easy to assign the same set of sound generator settings to more than one program number. You could, for instance, have one set of parameters assigned to even program numbers, and another set assigned to odd program numbers. You could then alternate between two sounds via the pedal. It is a very useful MIDI accessory for those who undertake 'live' performances, and it could also have its uses in a MIDI studio.

Circuit operation

The main circuit for the improved program change pedal is the same as that for the standard pedal (Figure 12.1), but the links to earth on pins 11 to 17 of IC7 are omitted. Pins 11 to 17 of IC7 are driven from the simple binary counter circuit of Figure 13.1. This is reset to zero at switch-on by the positive pulse produced by C9 and R13. A binary counter simply counts the number of pulses fed to its clock input, and produces the appropriate binary pattern on its outputs.

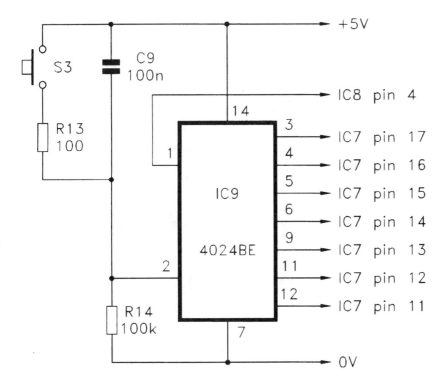

The clock input of IC9 (pin 1) is fed from pin 4 of IC4, which pulses at the end of each program change message. Therefore, IC9 feeds a value of zero to IC7 when the first byte is transmitted, and then it is incremented to one. A value of one is used in the data byte the next time S2 is operated, and at the end of that message IC9 is incremented to a count of two. Thus the counting action of IC9 results in the program number being incremented in the required manner. The count can be manually reset to zero at any time by operating S3.

At about 5 to 6 milliamps, the current consumption of this circuit is much the same as that of the basic program pedal circuit. As the binary counter is a CMOS type, and it is operating at a very low frequency, it produces a negligible increase in current consumption.

Construction

The first job is to build the main circuit board, which is a slightly modified version of the board for the original program change pedal. Figure 13.2 and 13.3 show the component layout and underside view of the modified stripboard. Like the original, it has 67 holes by 36 copper strips. This version of the board lacks some of the link wires to the right of IC7, but instead has solder pins here (including the one just to the left of IC8). In other respects construction of the board is

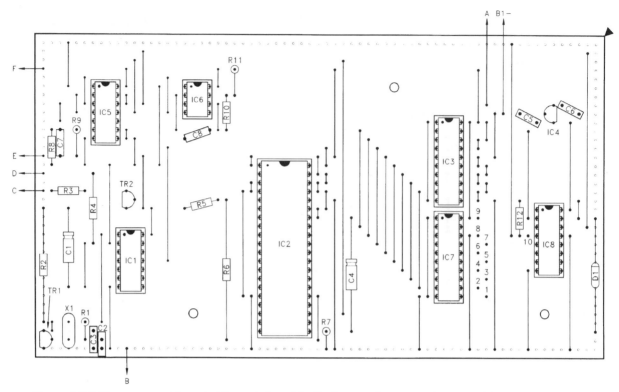

Figure 13.2 The component layout of the main board for the improved program change pedal

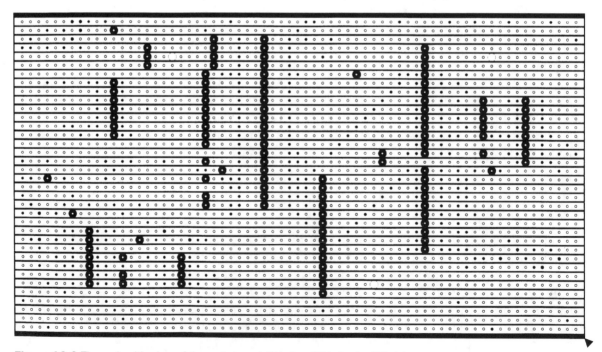

Figure 13.3 The underside view of the main board. This has 67 holes by 36 strips

exactly as before. The wiring to S1, S2, and SK1 is also exactly the same as before (see Figure 12.4).

The binary counter circuit is assembled onto a separate stripboard panel, and is connected to the main board via a piece of 10 way ribbon cable. Figure 13.4 shows the component layout for the counter board, plus the two connections to S3. The underside view of this board appears in Figure 13.5. Construction of this board is very simple, but remember that IC9 is a CMOS device which requires the usual anti-static handling precautions. The 10 way ribbon cable connects point '1' in Figure 13.2 to point '1' in Figure 13.4, point '2' to point '2', point '3' to point '3', and so on. I would recommend the use of multi-coloured 'rainbow' ribbon cable, rather than the all-grey variety. Mistakes are less likely using the multi-coloured type, and if a mistake should be made it will be much easier to trace.

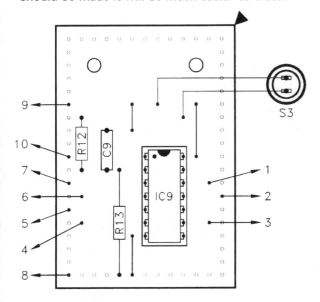

Figure 13.4 The component layout and wiring for the counter board

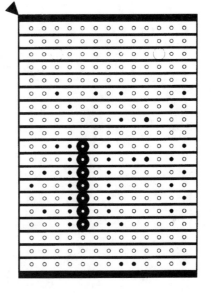

Figure 13.5 The underside of the counter board. This has 13 holes by 19 strips

User tips

The output socket of the pedal unit connects to the input socket of the synthesiser via a standard MIDI lead. Make sure that the synthesiser is set up to receive MIDI messages on channel 1, and then operate the foot-switch (S2). This should set the synthesiser to program 0. Try repeatedly operating the foot-switch to ensure that the synthesiser steps through program numbers 1, 2, 3, 4, etc. Pressing S3 resets the counter to zero, but this does not result in a program change message being sent. S2 must be operated in order to do this.

Sound assignment
In use it is advisable to have the various sounds assigned to program numbers 0, 1, 2, 3, etc. Using the pedal unit to set the synthesiser to program 0 will confirm that everything is functioning properly, and will set things ready for you to start playing.

Components

Resistors (all 0.25 watt 5% carbon film)

R1	1M
R2	2k2
R3	220R
R4	220R
R5	2k2
R6	6k8
R7	1k
R8	10k
R9	1M
R10	6k8
R11	47k
R12	68k
R13	100R
R14	100k

Capacitors

C1	100u 10V axial elect
C2	33p ceramic plate
C3	33p ceramic plate
C4	100u 10V axial elect
C5	100n disc ceramic
C6	100n disc ceramic
C7	10n polyester
C8	10n polyester
C9	100n polyester

Semiconductors

IC1	4024BE
IC2	6402 UART (or equivalent)
IC3	74HC245
IC4	uA78L05 (5V 100mA positive regulator)
IC5	4001BE
IC6	TLC555CP (or equivalent)
IC7	74HC245
IC8	4017BE
IC9	4024BE
TR1	BC549
TR2	BC559
D1	1N4148

Miscellaneous

B1   9 volt (PP3 size)
SK1 5 pin 180 degree DIN socket
S1   s.p.s.t. min toggle switch
S2   heavy duty non-locking push button switch (see text)
S3   Push to make, release to break, push button switch
X1   2MHz HC-49/U crystal
      Stripboard 67 holes by 36 strips and 13 holes by 19 strips
      battery connector
      8 pin DIL i.c. holder
      14 pin DIL i.c. holder (3 off)
      16 pin DIL i.c. holder
      20 pin DIL i.c. holder (2 off)
      40 pin DIL i.c. holder
      Medium size metal case
      10 way ribbon cable

Basic mixer

The term 'audio mixer' tends to conjure up images of massive consoles with bank after bank of slider controls. However, few of us really need a mixer having that degree of sophistication. In fact a very basic mixer is adequate in many situations. Often all that is needed is a very simple unit that will enable the outputs of three or four instruments to drive the input of a power amplifier. It is not even necessary to have a 'fader' control for each input, since the volume controls of the instruments can be used to balance the signal levels.

The simple mixer featured here has four inputs, but it is easily extended to have eight or more channels if you wish. It is presented in two versions, one of which is a very basic unit which lacks fader controls. The second version has a fader for each channel. The addition of faders makes the mixer more convenient to use, and it is essential to use this version of the unit if some of the signal sources lack output level controls.

Basic audio mixer

Circuit operation

Figure 14.1 shows the circuit diagram for the basic version of the mixer. This is a conventional operational amplifier summing mode mixer circuit. IC1 is used in what is really just a standard inverting mode amplifier circuit, but with four input resistors and d.c. blocking capacitors (R1 to R4 and C2 to C5 respectively). This works in much

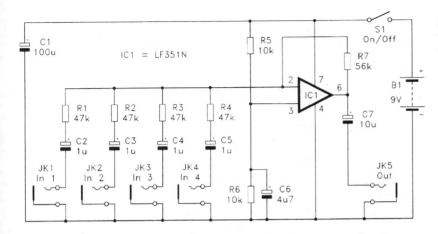

Figure 14.1 The circuit diagram
for the basic mixer. JK1 to JK4 are
the four input sockets

the same way as a simple inverting mode circuit, but the output responds to the sum of the input voltages, giving the desired mixing effect. The value of feedback resistor R5 sets the voltage gain from each input to the output at slightly more than unity.

The negative feedback action of the circuit stabilises the voltage at pin 2 of IC1, and produces what is called a 'virtual earth' here. This is important in a mixer application since it effectively isolates the inputs from one another. In the basic mixer circuit it is not essential to have this isolation, but it is very important in the version of Figure 14.2, which includes a volume control style fader potentiometer at each input. The almost total isolation between the inputs ensures that adjustment of one fader control has no significant effect on the other channels of the mixer.

With both versions of the circuit there is no difficulty in adding extra inputs. For the basic mixer it is just a matter of adding an extra 47k input resistor, 1u coupling capacitor, and jack socket for each additional channel. Of course, for the version which includes the fader

Figure 14.2 The version of the mixer that includes a 'fader' potentiometer at each input

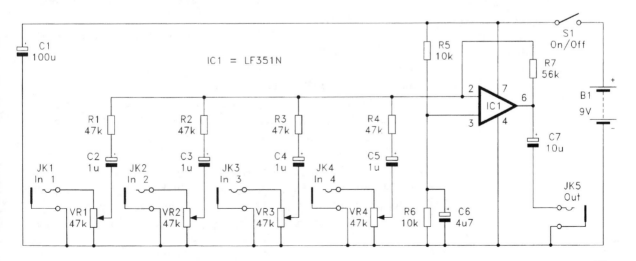

controls a 47k potentiometer is needed for each channel.

Readers often enquire about the maximum number of channels that can be used with a circuit of this type. There is not really a 'hard and fast' answer to this. Each additional input results in the noise level of IC1 increasing slightly, and a general reduction in its performance. Also, it results in more input wiring, which in turn increases the risk of a significant amount of mains 'hum' and other electrical noise being picked up in the input wiring. Provided the unit is housed in a metal case which gives good screening against stray pick up of electrical noise there should be no difficulty in having as many as ten channels. It may be acceptable to have more channels, but this is dependent on the level of performance that you are willing to accept.

The current consumption of the circuit is only about 2 milliamps or so. A PP3 size battery is therefore perfectly adequate as the power source, and each battery should have a very long operating life.

Construction

Whichever version of the unit you intend to build, the component panel illustrated in Figures 14.3 and 14.4 must be built. This is based on a stripboard which has 36 holes by 20 copper strips. Construction of this board is very straightforward and should not present any difficulties. IC1 can be any single low noise bifet operational amplifier (LF351N, TLO71CP, TLO81CP, etc.). These have Jfet input stages, and are not static-sensitive components.

Details of the point-to-point wiring for the basic mixer are provided in Figure 14.5. Figure 14.6 shows the hard wiring for the version of the circuit which includes fader potentiometers. In both cases there is no need to use screened leads to carry the connections from the sockets/potentiometers to the circuit board provided these leads are kept quite short.

For an audio project such as this it is advisable to use a case of all-metal construction that will provide overall screening against stray pick up of mains 'hum' and other electrical noise. The case should be earthed to the 0 volt supply rail of the mixer circuit. This connection will be carried via the jack sockets provided these are of open construction. The insulated variety (which have plastic bodies) will not provide an automatic earth connection to the case. If you use sockets of this type it would be advisable to connect the earth tag of one socket to a solder tag bolted on the inside of the case.

The wiring in Figure 14.6 is for rotary potentiometers. Many users prefer to use slider potentiometers in mixer applications. From the electronic point of view there is no difficulty in using slider poten-

More inputs

If more than four inputs are required the board must be extended by six holes per additional input. The extra input resistors, coupling capacitors, and pairs of solder pins are then added to the board using exactly the same layout as for the other input stages. Don't forget the additional two breaks in the copper strips for each extra set of input components.

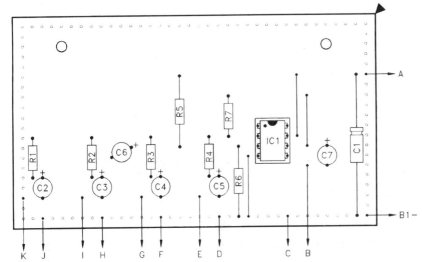

Figure 14.3 The component layout for the mixer board. The same board is used for both versions of the mixer

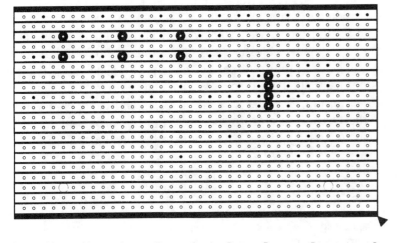

Figure 14.4 The underside of the mixer board. This measures 36 holes by 20 strips

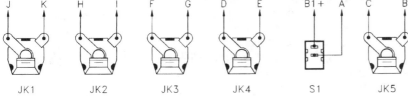

Figure 14.5 The hard wiring for the basic version of the mixer

tiometers, but there one or two general points to bear in mind. The first is simply that these controls are not as widely available as they were a few years ago. However, they are listed in some of the larger mail order component catalogues. These also list matching control knobs. Slider potentiometers tend to need quite a lot of panel space, even if you opt for small types having about 50 to 60 millimetres of travel. There is probably little point in using slider potentiometers unless you fit the mixer into a case of the sloping front variety.

Figure 14.6 The point-to-point wiring for the version of the mixer which includes 'fader' controls

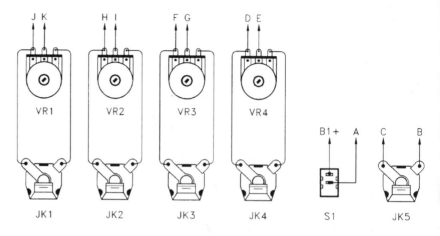

Slider potentiometers require a slit in the front panel to accommodate the control shaft. This can be cut using a miniature file, or 'needle' file as they are often called. Slider potentiometers usually have provision for a couple of short M2 mounting screws. The exact mounting arrangements vary somewhat from one make to another though, so it is advisable to check the retailer's literature before drilling any holes in the front panel! The tags of a slider potentiometer are normally numbered from '1' to '3' on the rear plate. Tag '1' goes to earth, tag '2' is the wiper connection, and tag '3' is the top end of the track. These are respectively the equivalents of the left hand, middle, and right hand potentiometer tags in Figure 14.6.

User tips

The output socket of the mixer connects to the audio power amplifier (or whatever) via a screened audio lead. This will usually be a lead having a 6.35 millimetre jack plug at each end, but this is obviously dependent on the type of input socket fitted on the amplifier. Testing the basic version of the mixer circuit is just a matter of connecting the output of an instrument to each of the input sockets, and then checking that each input signal is coupled through to the output correctly. Again, screened leads should be used, and it will probably be standard jack leads that are required.

If overloading occurs, with a distorted output signal being produced, one possible solution to the problem is to power the circuit from two 9 volt batteries wired in series. This gives the circuit greatly increased 'headroom'.

Alternatively, making R7 lower in value will reduce the gain of the circuit, and should keep the output signal down to a level that gives low distortion levels. Of course, if the signal sources have output level controls, these can be used to attenuate the output signals to levels that avoid distortion. With most electronic musical instruments the output levels are unlikely to give any problems with overloading.

Testing the version of the unit which has the fader controls is much the same as testing the basic unit. However, you should ensure that the fader controls operate properly. Of course, with this version of the unit there is no risk of overloading provided you are careful to use fader control settings that keep the input signals down to acceptable levels.

Components (Basic mixer)

Resistors (all 0.25 watt 5% carbon film)

R1	47k
R2	47k
R3	47k
R4	47k
R5	10k
R6	10k
R7	56k

Capacitors

C1	100u 10V axial elect
C2	1u 63V radial elect
C3	1u 63V radial elect
C4	1u 63V radial elect
C5	1u 63V radial elect
C6	4u7 63V radial elect
C7	10u 25V radial elect

Semiconductor

IC1	LF351N or similar

Miscellaneous

S1	s.p.s.t. min toggle switch
B1	9 volt (PP3 size)
JK1 to JK5	Standard (6.35mm) jack sockets (5 off)
	Medium size metal case
	Stripboard 36 holes by 20 strips
	Battery connector
	8 pin DIL i.c. holder

For the version which includes the fader controls a full set of basic mixer components are required, plus the following:

Potentiometers

VR1 to VR4   47k log (4 off)

Miscellaneous

Control knob (4 off)

15 | Stereo mixer

Figure 15.1 shows the circuit diagram for a stereo version of the audio mixer. This is basically just two mixer circuits of the type described previously, one for each stereo channel. Two-gang potentiometers are used for the fader controls, so that the levels of the stereo channels can be adjusted in unison. The only other significant difference between the stereo and mono mixer circuits is the inclusion of balance controls in the stereo version. The balance controls are VR2, VR4, VR6 and VR8. These are two-gang potentiometers which are used in series with the input resistors. The two gangs are wired out-of-phase (i.e. increasing the value of one gang gives a reduction in the resistance of the other gang). This permits a small imbalance in the gains of the two stereo channels to be introduced in order to counteract an imbalance in the two input levels.

The current consumption of the circuit is about 4 milliamps. A small (PP3 size) battery is therefore adequate as the power source.

Figure 15.1 The circuit diagram for the stereo version of the mixer

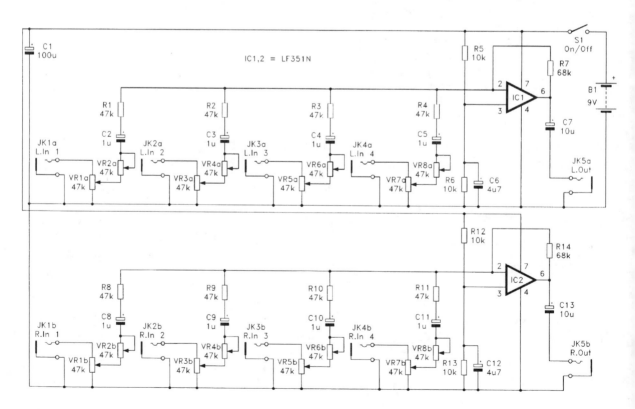

Stereo mixer board

Construction

Figure 15.2 and Figure 15.3 respectively show the component layout and underside of the stripboard. This has 37 holes by 39 copper strips. The hard wiring is shown in Figure 15.4. This might look rather complex at first sight, but it is basically just a small set of interconnections repeated four times (one for each stereo input). The wiring is really quite easy provided you take your time. The upper sets of three tags represent those for the front gangs of the potentiometers - the lower sets represent those for the rear sections. The input sockets are shown as separate (mono) jack sockets for each stereo channel. Of course, you can use stereo jacks, DIN sockets, or any audio connectors that will better suit your particular electronic music system.

User tips
The unit is tested in much the same way as the mono version, but obviously stereo sources must be used. Note that the balance controls only permit a moderate degree of imbalance to be introduced, which is all that should be required in practice. If a stereo signal source provides signals that are at very different levels, that piece of equipment is almost certainly faulty, or incorrectly set up.

Stereo and mono
You may wish to use a mixture of stereo and mono signal sources. One way of using a mono signal source with this mixer is to simply feed the signal to one stereo channel. This will place that signal fully on one side of the stereo sound stage or the other. The alternative, and what will normally be the better course of action, is to feed the mono source into both stereo channels. The relevant balance control will then act as a pan control, and will enable the signal to be positioned at the desired point in the sound stage.

Figure 15.2 The component layout for the stereo mixer. The board measures 37 holes by 39 strips

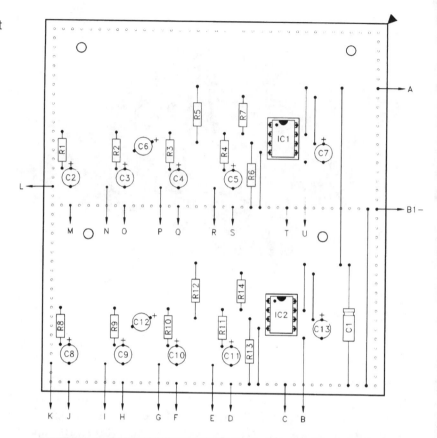

Figure 15.3 The underside of the stereo mixer board

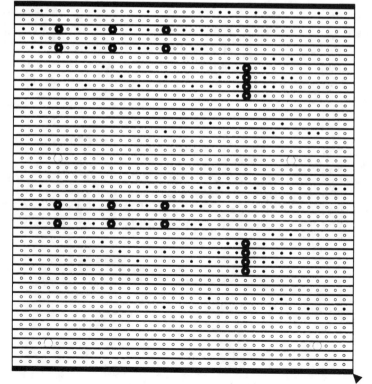

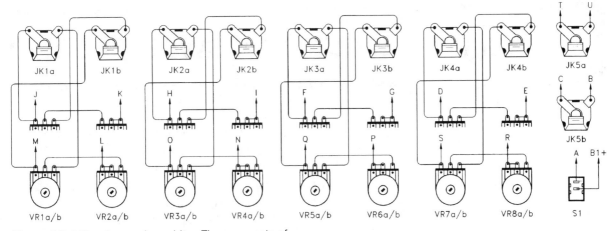

Figure 15.4 The stereo mixer wiring. The upper sets of potentiometer tags represent those for the front gangs

Components (Stereo mixer)

Resistors (all 0.25 watt 5% carbon film)

R1	47k
R2	47k
R3	47k
R4	47k
R5	10k
R6	10k
R7	68k
R8	47k
R9	47k
R10	47k
R11	47k
R12	10k
R13	10k
R14	68k

Potentiometers

VR1	47k log dual gang
VR2	47k lin dual gang
VR3	47k log dual gang
VR4	47k lin dual gang
VR5	47k log dual gang
VR6	47k lin dual gang
VR7	47k log dual gang
VR8	47k lin dual gang

Capacitors

C1	100u 10V axial elect
C2	1u 63V radial elect
C3	1u 63V radial elect
C4	1u 63V radial elect
C5	1u 63V radial elect
C6	4u7 63V radial elect
C7	10u 25V radial elect
C8	1u 63V radial elect
C9	1u 63V radial elect
C10	1u 63V radial elect
C11	1u 63V radial elect
C12	4u7 63V radial elect
C13	10u 25V radial elect

Semiconductor

IC1	LF351N or similar
IC2	LF351N or similar

Miscellaneous

S1	s.p.s.t. min toggle switch
B1	9 volt (PP3 size)
JK1 to JK5	Standard (6.35mm) jack sockets (10 off, see text)
	Large size metal case
	Stripboard 37 holes by 39 strips
	Battery connector
	8 pin DIL i.c. holder (2 off)
	Control knob (8 off)

16 Electronic swell pedal

T his simple project is an electronic alternative to a conventional swell pedal. It does not actually have a pedal, but is instead controlled via two foot operated switches. Operating one switch causes a rise in volume until the maximum level is reached. Operating the other switch has the opposite effect, with the volume steadily diminishing until the input signal is completely faded out. The volume setting is immediately 'frozen' when a switch is released. Using the switches you can therefore raise or lower the volume control setting to the desired point, and then hold it at that setting until another change is required.

Electronic swell pedal

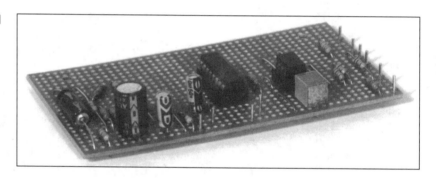

Circuit operation

Refer to Figure 16.1 for the electronic swell pedal circuit diagram. The circuit really breaks down into two sections. On the left there is a voltage controlled amplifier (v.c.a.) based on IC1. This is one section of an LM13600N dual transconductance operational amplifier. Although this is a form of operational amplifier, it does not really have much in common with the 741C and other conventional operational amplifiers. It is a current rather than voltage operated device, and it has an input at pin 1 which can be used to control its gain. Strictly speaking, the circuit is a current controlled amplifier rather than a voltage controlled type, but the inclusion of R9 in series with the control current input effectively converts the circuit to voltage control. The higher the control voltage, the higher the current that will flow through R9 and into pin 1 of IC1.

The right hand section of the circuit provides the v.c.a. with suit-

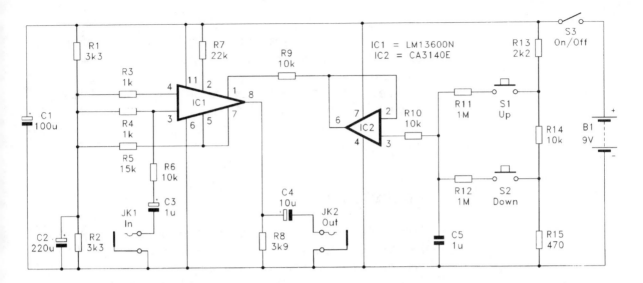

Figure 16.1 The electronic swell pedal circuit diagram. Only one section of IC1 is used in this circuit

able control voltages. C5 is in an uncharged state at switch-on, and it therefore feeds zero volts to the input of the buffer amplifier based on IC2. Operating S1 results in C5 charging from the supply rail via R11 and R13.

Due to the high value of R11, it takes a few seconds before the charge on C5 rises to something approaching the maximum achievable potential. When S1 is opened again, the charge on C5 will remain unchanged for a considerable period of time. The charge potential will gradually diminish over a period of time due to leakage resistances.

A non-electrolytic capacitor is used for C5 because a capacitor of this type can be relied upon to have an extremely high leakage resistance. An operational amplifier having a MOS input stage is used in the IC2 position, and this ensures that the input resistance of the buffer stage is too high to significantly discharge C5.

The charge voltage will eventually reduce, or it could even increase. This really depends on the leakage resistances in the circuit board, and the quality of C5. However, the voltage should remain reasonably stable over a period of many minutes, which is all that is required for good results in the present application. The charge on C5 can be deliberately leaked away by operating S2. The high value of R12 produces a slow decay over a period of a few seconds. Therefore, operating S1 produces a rise in gain through IC1, up to the point where maximum gain is achieved.

Operating S2 steadily reduces the gain back to zero. The audio input signal can therefore be 'faded' up using S1, and faded down again using S2. When neither switch is being operated, the volume level will be held at its current level for a long time.

C5 is driven from a potential divider (R13 to R15) rather than direct from the supply rails. This keeps the charge on C5 within the operating range of the rest of the circuit. This avoids delays between the pedal switches being operated and any change in volume being produced.

The current consumption of the circuit is about 5 milliamps. A PP3 size battery will have a reasonably long operating life, but it would be better to use a higher capacity type if the unit is likely to be used for long periods.

Construction

Details of the stripboard for the electronic swell pedal are provided in Figures 16.2 (top side) and 16.3 (underside). The point-to-point wiring is shown in Figure 16.4. The stripboard has 43 holes by 22 copper strips. Construction of the board offers nothing out of the ordinary, but remember that the CA3140E used for IC2 has a PMOS input stage. Accordingly, it requires the normal anti-static handling precautions.

Note that C5 must be a miniature printed circuit mounting type if it is to fit onto the board properly. Ideally it should have a lead spacing of 10 millimetres (0.4 inches). It might be possible to fit a larger type onto the board diagonally, but some 1u non-electrolytic capacitors are simply too big to fit onto the board. I would not recommend the use of an electrolytic capacitor as these have relatively high leakage levels, and might not hold the set volume levels for very long. Some component retailers sell the LM13700N rather than the LM13600N. These two components seem to be virtually identical, and both devices will operate properly in this circuit.

The mechanical side of construction needs to be carefully thought out if the unit is to be useable. S1 and S2 are large push-button switches of the non-locking variety (i.e. the contacts close when the push-buttons are pressed, and open again when they are released). Probably the best arrangement is to have a sloping front case with only the two switches mounted on the front panel. They should be positioned several inches apart so that it is easy to operate one switch without accidentally pressing the other one as well. Whatever layout you adopt, it will take a little practice before you can use the unit intuitively. Unless a sensible layout is used, you will never get to the stage where the unit can be used with ease.

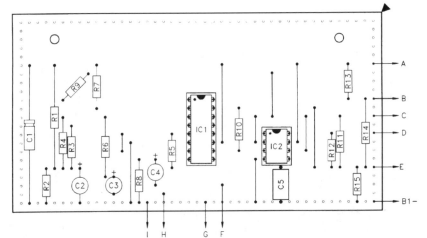

Figure 16.2 The component layout for the electronic swell pedal board

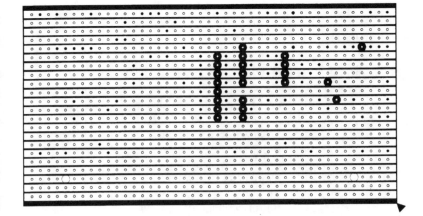

Figure 16.3 The underside of the swell pedal board. This has 43 holes by 22 strips

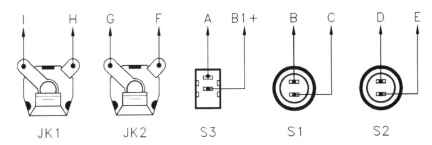

Figure 16.4 The electronic swell pedal wiring

User tips

In order to test the unit, connect it between a synthesiser (or whatever) and the audio amplifier system. Ordinary screened jack leads are used to provide these connections. Initially the unit will almost certainly block the signal due to a lack of any initial charge on C5. Operating S1 should enable the output signal to be brought up to something roughly comparable to the input level, and by operating S1 and S2 it should then be possible to raise or lower the volume of the instrument, as required.

The speed at which the volume rises is controlled by the value of R11. Similarly, the rate at which the volume falls is governed by the value of R12.

The time taken for the signal to rise or fall in level is proportional to the value of the appropriate resistor. For example, the time taken for the volume to rise from zero to maximum can be roughly halved by reducing the value of R11 to 470k. The values of R11 and R12 do not have to be the same, so it is possible to have totally different rise and fall rates.

The rise and fall times can be made variable by replacing R11 and R12 with 2M2 variable resistances. Replacing each one with a 2M2 potentiometer in series with a 220k fixed resistor should give good results.Volume fall is governed by the value of R12.

Components (Electronic swell pedal)

Resistors (all 0.25 watt 5% carbon film)

R1	3k3
R2	3k3
R3	1k
R4	1k
R5	15k
R6	10k
R7	22k
R8	3k9
R9	10k
R10	10k
R11	1M
R12	1M
R13	2k2
R14	10k
R15	470R

Capacitors

C1	100u 10V axial elect
C2	220u 10V radial elect
C3	1u 63 V radial elect
C4	10u 25V radial elect
C5	1u polystyrene (10mm lead spacing)

Semiconductors

IC1	LM13600N or LM13700N
IC2	CA3140E

Miscellaneous

S1	Large non-locking push-button switch
S2	Large non-locking push-button switch
S3	s.p.s.t. min toggle switch
JK1	Standard (6.35mm) jack socket
JK2	Standard (6.35mm) jack socket
B1	9 volt (PP3 size)
	Metal case (see text)
	Stripboard 43 holes by 22 strips
	Battery connector
	8 pin DIL i.c. holder
	16 pin DIL i.c. holder

Metronome   17

F or well over a hundred years metronomes were purely mechanical devices having a clockwork mechanism. These were sometimes known as Maelzel's metronomes, after their inventor. They have a swinging arm, and produce 'clicking' sounds at regular intervals. The 'click' rate is usually adjustable from about 30 beats per minute to around ten times that figure. Although mechanical metronomes are still used quite widely, they are starting to become collectors items. New metronomes are now virtually all of the electronic variety. They vary considerably in sophistication, but they all provide the same basic function as the original metronomes. The metronome featured here is an extremely simple device which produces 'click' sounds from a miniature loudspeaker. Each 'click' is accompanied by a flash from a LED on the front panel. It has a beat rate which is adjustable from about 30 to 300 beats per minute via a calibrated control knob.

Circuit operation

As can be seen from the circuit diagram of Figure 17.1, this metronome is a very simple device. It is basically just a standard 555

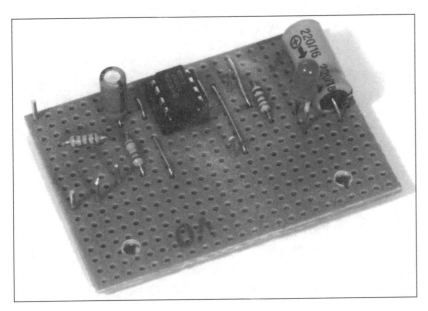

Metronome circuit board

Figure 17.1 The metronome circuit diagram. VR1 provides a beat range of about 30 to 300 per minute

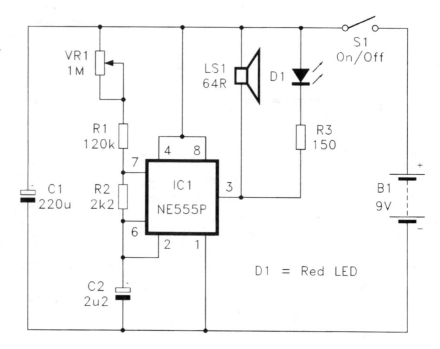

oscillator circuit. In order to produce the required 'click' sounds it is necessary to feed the loudspeaker with brief pulses. A pulse duration of well under a millisecond is needed in order to give suitable high-pitched 'click' sounds. This is one application where the 555s unequal mark-space ratio is a definite advantage, as it makes it easy to set a suitable output waveform. The output at pin 3 of IC1 is high while C2 is being charged via VR1, R1, R2. VR1 enables the charge time to be varied from approximately 2 seconds at maximum value to about 0.2 seconds at minimum value. This equates to the beat rate range of 30 to 300 per minute that was mentioned previously.

The output of IC1 goes low while C2 is being discharged. It is discharged through R2 and an internal switching transistor of IC1. R2 therefore controls the time for which the output pulses low, and its low value provides a suitably short pulse duration. LS1 is connected between the output of IC1 and the positive supply rail so that it is fed with a large pulse of current each time IC1's output goes low. D1 is the LED indicator, and together with its current limiting resistor (R3) it is connected in parallel with LS1. It therefore switches on briefly each time LS1 produces a 'click' sound. The high value of supply decoupling capacitor C1 ensures that the high currents drawn by LS1 and D1 can be supplied properly.

Due to the brief and intermittent nature of the output signal, plus the high values in the timing circuit, the current consumption of the circuit is little more than the current consumed by IC1. This is approximately 8 milliamps. A PP3 size battery is just about adequate to supply this, but a higher capacity battery is likely to be a more economic means of powering the unit. The current consumption can be greatly reduced by using a low power version of the 555 timer for IC1, but low power 555s do not always work well in a circuit of this type, where the output is providing high output currents. I would therefore recommend using the standard version.

Construction

The metronome stripboard measures 24 holes by 17 copper strips. Figure 17.2 shows the component layout and Figure 17.3 shows the underside view. Details of the point-to-point wiring are shown in Figure 17.4. The component panel is very simple to build, but there are a couple of points which are worthy of note. Although D1 is shown as being mounted on the circuit board, as only a single LED is involved in this case it is probably easier to mount it off-board in a panel holder, and then hard wire it to the circuit board. D1 is pulsed at quite a high current, but it is only switched on very briefly. It is therefore advisable to use a high brightness LED so that really good LED brightness is obtained.

C2 needs to be a high quality capacitor, and an ordinary electrolytic is unlikely to give good results. The tolerances on electrolytics are usually quite large, and they often have quite high leakage levels. This could result in the beat range of the unit being very inaccurate. The circuit might even fail to operate at all at some settings of VR1. C2 can be a high quality electrolytic capacitor, but a tantalum bead type is probably a safer choice.

Fixing LS1 on the rear of the front panel could be slightly awkward, since few miniature loudspeakers have provision for screw fixing. I usually start by drilling the front panel with a matrix of holes about four to five millimetres in diameter. Provided this is done neatly it produces quite a good speaker grille. The loudspeaker is then glued in place behind the grille using any good quality general purpose adhesive. Use the adhesive very sparingly, and only apply it to the front rim of the loudspeaker, being careful not to smear the diaphragm. LS1 can be any moving coil loudspeaker which has an impedance of about 40 ohms or more. One having a diameter of about 70 to 80 millimetres is likely to give better volume than one of about 50 millimetres in diameter.

Figure 17.2 The component layout for the metronome circuit board

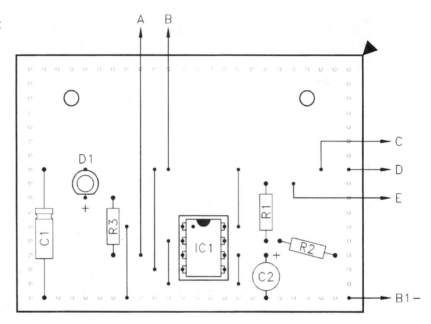

Figure 17.3 The underside of the metronome board. This measures 24 holes by 17 strips

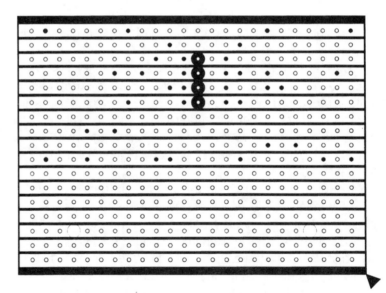

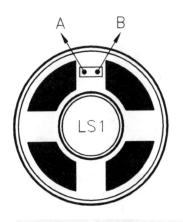

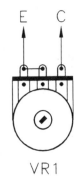

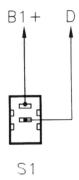

Figure 17.4 The metronome point-to-point wiring

User tips

When switched on the unit should produce a series of 'clicks', and D1 should flash quite brightly. Check that VR1 controls the beat rate correctly.

If the unit is to be of any real use the control knob of VR1 must be equipped with a scale calibrated in beats per minute. In order to obtain reasonable accuracy it is necessary for the scale to be reasonably large, which in turn dictates that the control knob should be a large type. The calibration points can be marked using rub-on transfers. Finding the calibration process is likely to be a long process, since it involves a fair amount of trial and error. The beat rate can be determined by simply counting the number of beats in a one minute period. In order to save time it is probably best to count the number of beats in a 15 second period, and then multiply by four in order to convert this into beats per minute. This should still give accurate results, although at the lowest rates it might be better to use a 30 second measuring period and multiply by two in order to give an answer in beats per minute.

Components (Metronome)

Resistors (all 0.25 watt 5% carbon film)

R1   120k
R2   2k2
R3   150R

Potentiometer

VR1   1M lin carbon

Capacitors

C1   220u 10V axial elect
C2   2u2 50V tantalum bead (see text)

Semiconductors

IC1   NE555P
D1   5mm high brightness red LED

Miscellaneous

S1   s.p.s.t. min toggle switch
B1   9 volt (6 x HP7 size cells in plastic holder)
LS1   64R 70mm diameter loudspeaker (see text)
Small metal or plastic case
Stripboard 24 holes by 17 strips
8 pin DIL i.c. holder
PP3 battery connector
Control knob
Panel holder for D1

18 Analogue echo unit

T hese days digital effects units represent the best means of obtaining effects that require an audio signal to be delayed. They certainly represent the best means of obtaining effects that require long delay times, such as echo and reverberation types. Unfortunately, digital delay line circuits are still relatively complex, and expensive to build. There are numerous ways of delaying an audio signal, but most methods only give very short delays.

For an echo effect, a delay of at least 60 milliseconds is required, which in electronic terms is something not far short of an eternity. The only type of circuit capable of producing delays of this magnitude at reasonably low cost is an analogue delay line of the 'bucket brigade' variety. These are actually quite complex circuits, but there are several delay line integrated circuits available. These enable a variety of delay times to be obtained using relatively few components. A delay of 60 milliseconds or so with a reasonably wide bandwidth is just about achievable using the longest bucket brigade devices.

Bucket brigade delay line chips are actually charge coupled devices (c.c.d.s). They are basically just dozens of capacitors and electronic switches plus some control circuitry. The capacitors hold electrical charges, and are analogous to a bucket holding water. In the bucket brigade analogy there is a line of buckets and X amount of water is placed into the first of these. The first bucket is then emptied into the second one, which is in turn emptied into the third bucket. Meanwhile, Y amount of water is poured into the first bucket. Its contents are then emptied into bucket number two, and at the same time the water in bucket number three is poured into the fourth bucket.

This process is continued until X and Y amounts of water reach the end of the bucket brigade and are discarded. In fact a continuous stream of water samples are taken in at the input, and after a delay each one completes the journey along the chain of buckets and appears at the output.

In a real c.c.d. delay line it is the input voltage that is sampled, and the sampled voltages are fed along a chain of capacitors via electronic switches. There is a slight problem with this system in that the last stage can not simultaneously provide an output signal and receive a sample from the previous stage. This results in a pulsed output waveform which can actually be filtered to recover the original audio signal. However, it requires a massive amount of filtering in order to do this properly. Practical delay lines normally have an extra stage which maintains the output signal during the periods when the final delaying stage is receiving a new sample. Some filtering is still needed in order to remove the steps in the output waveform that inevitably occur with a sampling system. Reasonably simple filtering is sufficient to do this though.

Even fairly modest delays require a c.c.d. chip having a few hundred stages, and the relatively long delay time needed for an echo effect requires more than three thousand stages. The chip used in this circuit is an MN3011 which has some 3328 stages.

Circuit operation

The full circuit diagram for the analogue echo unit appears in Figure 18.1. IC3 is the bucket brigade chip, and this has outputs available from various stages along the delay line in addition to an output from the final stage. In this application it is only the final output that is required, and the other five outputs of IC3 are left unconnected. R8 is a load resistor for the final output stage. The delay time is determined by the number of stages in the delay line, and the rate at which samples are moved from one capacitor to the next. The sampling rate is controlled by an external clock oscillator based on IC5. This provides IC3 with a two-phase clock signal plus an accurate bias voltage.

Figure 18.1 The analogue echo unit circuit diagram. IC3 is the bucket brigade delay line chip

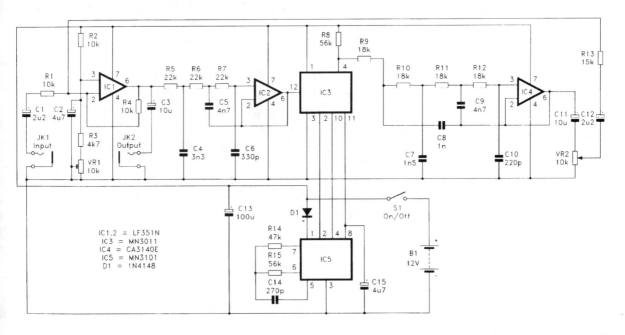

The clock frequency is set at just over 16kHz by the C - R timing network. The delay time (in milliseconds) is obtained by dividing the number of delaying stages by twice the clock frequency (in kilohertz). In this case the delay time is obviously about 100 milliseconds, which is more than adequate to give an echo effect.

IC4 is used as the basis of an active fourth order (24dB per octave) lowpass filter which removes the steps in the output signal from IC3. In order to obtain good results the sample frequency must be at least double the maximum frequency handled by the delay line. Ideally it would be three or more times higher than the maximum signal frequency. The output filter has a cutoff frequency of about 5kHz, which ensures that the delay line will function properly. On the other hand, it clearly gives substantially less than the full audio bandwidth. Fortunately, it is only the echo signal which has the limited bandwidth, and the straight-through signal has the full audio bandwidth. A bandwidth of 5kHz for the echo signal is sufficient to give good results.

IC2 is used in a third order (18dB per octave) lowpass filter at the input of the delay line. This removes strong input signals at frequencies close to the clock frequency. This would otherwise produce severe distortion. IC1 is used as a mixer stage which combines the straight-through and delayed signals. VR2 is a variable attenuator which controls the strength of the delayed signal fed back to the mixer stage. As the delayed signal is fed back to the input of the circuit, it circulates around the circuit, gradually decaying to nothing. This gives a multiple echo effect, with the echoes gradually dying away. VR2 controls both the strength of the initial echo, and the time taken for the echoes to decay to an insignificant level. The higher the setting of VR2, the longer it takes for signals to decay to an insignificant level.

VR1 enables the bias level of the circuit to be adjusted for optimum large signal handling. Although VR1 controls the biasing of the entire circuit, it is the biasing of the delay line that must be set for optimum results, and which limits the maximum level that can be accommodated properly. A signal of several volts peak-to-peak can be handled with VR1 set correctly.

The current consumption of the circuit is approximately 9 milliamps from a 12 volt supply. The battery consists of eight HP7 size cells in a plastic holder, and these have a very long operating life. The circuit will almost certainly work quite well on a 9 volt supply, but with some loss of dynamic range.

Construction

The component side and underside views of the stripboard panel are shown in Figures 18.2 and 18.3 respectively. The point-to-point wiring is illustrated in Figure 18.4. The board has 60 holes by 30 copper strips. This is a fairly complex project, and even experienced constructors need to take due care when constructing the circuit

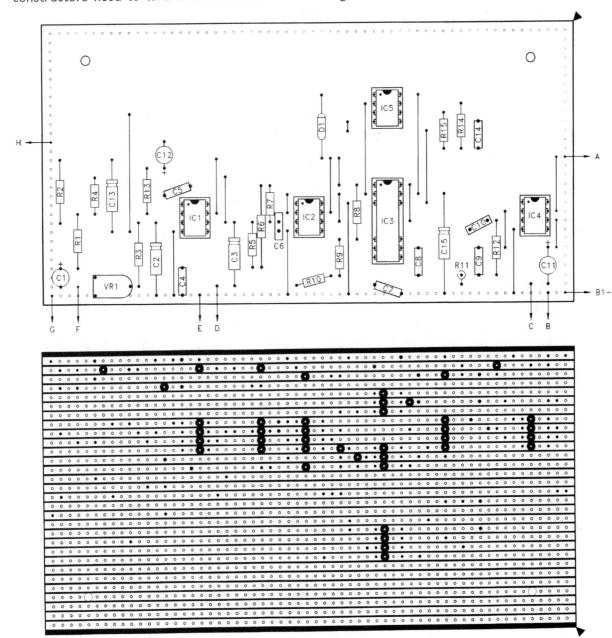

Figure 18.3 The underside of the echo unit board

board. It is a project which is not really suitable for those of limited project building experience.

IC3, IC4, and IC5 are MOS devices which require the standard anti-static handling precautions. These should be scrupulously observed when dealing with IC3, since the MN3011 is quite an expensive device. The MN3011 has an unusual encapsulation which is a 12 pin DIL type. This is basically an 18 pin DIL encapsulation, but with the middle three pins of each row omitted. It is unlikely that a 12 pin DIL holder will be obtainable, but it will fit into an ordinary 18 pin DIL type. I removed the six pins of the holder that are not required, but this is not strictly necessary. It simply gives a slightly neater looking result.

VR1 must be a miniature horizontal mounting preset if it is to fit into the component layout correctly. IC1 and IC2 can be any low noise Bifet operational amplifiers (TL071CP, TL081CP, LF351N, etc.), and the standard 741C will also work quite well in this circuit. I would not recommend using anything other than a CA3140E for IC4 though. Other types will almost certainly result in severe clipping on negative half cycles, and a severely distorted output signal.

User tips

VR1 should be adjusted to a roughly mid-point setting initially, and this will probably provide quite good results. If suitable test gear is available, adjust VR1 to give symmetrical clipping at the output of IC4 using the normal procedures. If suitable test gear is not to hand, simply give VR1 any setting that provides a good quality output on high level signals. Note that VR1 has little effect on the quality of the straight-through signal, and that it is the quality of the echo signal that you are trying to optimise.

The echo unit is connected between the synthesiser (or other instrument) and the power amplifier using ordinary screened jack leads. In order to obtain a good signal to noise ratio it is essential that the instrument should provide a reasonably high output level. A signal level of around one volt r.m.s. is ideal. It will almost certainly be necessary to use a preamplifier to boost the input signal to an adequate level if the unit is used with something like a guitar having a low output pick-up. A preamplifier will certainly be needed if the unit is used with a microphone.

Try VR2 at various settings and listen to the difference it makes to the echo effect. In general it is best to use a middle setting. This gives a reasonably strong effect, but it avoids the problems that can occur at high settings. One of these is an inevitable build-up of noise, and a substantial reduction in the signal to noise ratio. Another is that the signal level tends to gradually build up, possibly resulting in overloading after a few seconds. A mid-setting gives better performance and what is usually a much better effect.

If a high pitched whistling sound can be heard on the output signal when VR2 is well advanced, this means that the clock frequency is too low. Reducing C14 to a value of 220p should cure this problem.

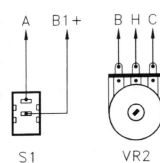 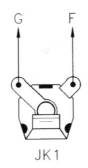 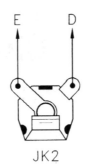

Figure 18.4 The echo unit point-to-point wiring

Components (Analogue echo unit)

Resistors (all 0.25 watt 5% carbon film)

R1	10k
R2	10k
R3	4k7
R4	10k
R5	22k
R6	22k
R7	22k
R8	56k
R9	18k
R10	18k
R11	18k
R12	18k
R13	15k
R14	47k
R15	56k

Potentiometers

VR1	10k sub min hor preset
VR2	10k log carbon

Capacitors

C1	2u2 63V radial elect
C2	4u7 63V axial elect
C3	10u 25V axial elect
C4	3n3 polyester
C5	4n7 polyester
C6	330p ceramic plate
C7	1n5 polyester
C8	1n polyester
C9	4n7 polyester
C10	220p ceramic plate
C11	10u 25V radial elect
C12	2u2 63V radial elect
C13	100u 16V axial elect
C14	270p ceramic plate
C15	4u7 63V axial elect

Semiconductors

IC1	LF351N
IC2	LF351N
IC3	MN3011
IC4	CA3140E
IC5	MN3101
D1	1N4148

Miscellaneous

JK1	Standard (6.35mm) jack socket
JK2	Standard (6.35mm) jack socket
S1	s.p.s.t. min toggle
B1	12 volt (8 x HP7 size cells in plastic holder)

Medium size metal case
Stripboard 60 holes by 30 strips
8 pin DIL i.c. holder (4 off)
18 pin DIL i.c. holder
Control knob
PP3 type battery connector

Glossary

Amplitude modulation

This is where one signal varies the strength (amplitude) of another signal. In an electronic music context, a low frequency oscillator rhythmically varies the volume of an instrument to give the familiar tremolo effect.

Attenuate

If an electrical signal is made smaller, it is attenuated (e.g. if you back-off a volume control you are increasing the attenuation it provides.

Axial

Components which are tubular in shape and have a leadout wire coming from each end are axial types. Virtually all resistors and many capacitors are of this type.

Balanced line input

An input which has two terminals, neither of which are earths. This type of input combats unwanted pickup of electrical noise using a cancelling process. Screening is normally used as well, so as to give an extremely low level of stray pickup. This type of input is much used on professional mixing desks and other professional audio equipment. A direct injection (DI) box is needed in order to use a normal non-balanced signal source (which includes most guitars) with a balanced line input.

Bandpass filter

This is a circuit which only allows signals over a small range of frequencies to pass through to the output. Signals at other frequencies are greatly attenuated. Bandpass filtering is used to provide waa-waa effects.

Base

The name given to one of the terminals of a transistor.

Baud

This is the speed at which data is transmitted in a serial data system (such as MIDI). MIDI operates at 31250 baud (or 31.25 kilobaud), which means that with a continuous stream of data some 31250 bits of information per second are sent. This is not quite as good as it might at first appear, since ten bits (including timing bits) per byte are required, and typically three bytes per MIDI message are needed. This works out at around one thousand MIDI messages per second. This is adequate for most purposes, but with complex systems it is possible for MIDI to become overloaded.

Bifet

A term applied to integrated circuits which use a combination of ordinary (bipolar) and field effect transistors. Most devices of this type are operational amplifiers which are primarily intended for use in audio circuits. Devices of this type provide low noise and distortion levels.

Binary

A form of numbering system where the only digits used are 0 and 1. This may seem a bit crude, but it is the system used in all digital electronics, and MIDI sends values in the form of binary numbers.

Bit

Bit is an abbreviation for 'binary digit', which is the basic unit of information used in a digital system such as MIDI.

Bucket brigade device

A popular name for delay lines which work by passing electrical charges along a chain of capacitors. They are more correctly termed charge coupled devices (c.c.d.s).

Byte

Digital systems normally operate on 8 bits of data at a time, and a group of eight bits is a byte. Even with a system such as MIDI where bits are sent one at a time, they are still grouped into 8 bit bytes.

Capacitor

A common electronic component that can store an electrical charge. Normal capacitors can be connected either way round, but electrolytics and certain other polarised types must be connected with the correct polarity.

Carbon film
A type of resistor, and what is these days the 'standard' type.

Ceramic plate capacitor
These are miniature low value capacitors which are often only about 3 millimetres square and under a millimetre thick. They are not the highest quality components in some respects, but are adequate for most purposes.

Channel
MIDI can operate on up to sixteen channels that are normally simply called channels 1 to 16. Many MIDI messages carry a channel number, and can be selected by just one instrument (mode 3) or one voice of an instrument (mode 4). Note that any equipment set with 'omni on' will simply ignore channel numbers and respond to all messages.

Channel messages
These are simply the MIDI messages that carry a channel number in the header byte, and which can therefore be directed to one instrument, or one voice of an instrument. These messages include such things as note on, note off, and program change instructions. Messages that do not contain a channel number are called system messages.

Charge coupled device (c.c.d.)
See 'bucket brigade device'.

Chip
Modern semiconductors (transistors, integrated circuits, etc.) are basically chips of silicon. Any semiconductor component made from a silicon chip could be called a 'chip', but it is a term that is normally only applied to integrated circuits.

Clipping
This is where the peaks of a signal are chopped off, producing severe distortion. This occurs accidentally when an amplifier is over-driven, or deliberately to produce distortion, overdrive, and 'fuzz' effects (which are all terms for the same thing). Hard clipping simply chops off the signal peaks, while soft clipping gives a sort of rounding of the peaks. In terms of the sound produced, hard clipping gives much harsher distortion.

Clock
A clock signal (in electronic music) is a regular series of electronic pulses sent from one sequencer to another in order to keep the two units properly synchronised (a system which is mainly associated with drum machines). In a MIDI context the clock signal is a regular series of MIDI clock messages, rather than just a simple series of pulses. In general electronics a clock is an oscillator circuit that provides a regular series of pulses. Clock oscillators are often highly accurate and stable types which are controlled by a quartz crystal

CMOS
An acronym for 'complementary metal oxide silicon', a technology used in the production of some integrated circuits. These devices usually have very low current consumptions, and are static sensitive.

Collector
The name given to one of the terminals of a transistor.

Cutoff frequency
See Filtering

Delay line
A circuit which delays the signal passing through it by a certain length of time. Delay lines are used a great deal in electronic music and with electric guitars as several popular effects are based on them (echo, flanging, chorus, etc.).

DIN connector
There is a large range of DIN connectors for use in audio applications, computing, etc. In an electronic music context the 5 way 180 degree DIN connectors (also known as 5 pin type A DIN connectors) are the most important. These are the standard connectors used for MIDI inputs and outputs.

Diode
A simple electronic component which permits an electric current to flow in one direction, but not in the other. Diodes are semiconductors (like transistors and integrated circuits).

Direct injection (DI) box
See 'balanced line input'.

Disc ceramic

A type of capacitor, and one which is rather low in quality in some respects. However, disc ceramics have some qualities which make them ideal for certain applications.

Drain

The name given to one of the terminals of a field effect transistor (f.e.t.).

Dry joint

A soldered connection which does not provide a good electrical connection. A joint of this type will often be globular in appearance, possibly with a dull finish to the solder and a lot of burnt flux over and around the joint.

Dual in-line (d.i.l.)

Any component which has two identical rows of pins, side-by-side, is a dual in-line type. In practice it is mainly integrated circuits that have this type of pin arrangement, although it is used for a few other types of component.

E24 series

Resistors and capacitors are available only in certain values, popularly known as the E24 series (there being 24 values in each decade). Each value is very roughly 10% higher than the previous value. Some components are available only in every other value (the E12 series) or every fourth value (the E6 series).

Electrolytic

A type of capacitor. High value capacitors are mostly of the electrolytic variety. These are polarised capacitors which must be fitted the right way round if they are to function correctly.

Emitter

The name given to one of the terminals of a transistor.

Farad

Capacitance is measured in farads. A farad is a very large unit, and so most large capacitors have their value in marked in microfarads (millionths of a farad). Smaller capacitors have their values marked in nanofarads or picofarads. A nanofarad is one thousandth of a microfarad, and a picofarad is one thousandth of a nanofarad (or one millionth of a microfarad).

Field effect transistor (f.e.t.)

A type of transistor. F.e.t.s and ordinary bipolar transistors have very different characteristics, and are definitely not interchangeable.

Filtering (frequency)

An electronic filter is a circuit that lets signal at some frequencies pass unhindered, while other frequencies are greatly reduced in strength (attenuated). A lowpass filter attenuates frequencies above a certain frequency (the 'cutoff' frequency). A highpass filter attenuates signals below the cutoff frequency. A bandpass filter permits a narrow band of frequencies to pass, but attenuates all others. A notch filter attenuates frequencies over a narrow band, but lets all others pass unhindered.

Filtering (MIDI)

MIDI filtering is where a device is used to remove certain types of MIDI message. In practice the filtering is not usually provided by a separate processor connected into the MIDI signal path. It is usually provided by the built-in filtering of devices in the system. In other words, a device is set to ignore a certain type of message (e.g. pitch bend).

Flux

Solder for electrical and electronic use contains multiples cores of flux which help the solder to flow properly over the joint. This produces a good strong joint and a reliable electrical contact.

Frequency

Essentially another word for pitch. Frequency is expressed in hertz, and one hertz is one pressure wave, string vibration, or whatever, per second. Higher audio frequencies are measured in kilohertz (1000 hertz equals 1 kilohertz). The audio range is generally accepted as extending from 20 hertz to 20 kilohertz, although few people can actually hear the extremes of this range. The concert pitch middle A is at a frequency of 440 hertz.

Gain

Just another word for amplification.

Gate

The name given to one of the terminals of a field effect transistor (f.e.t.).

Gate

The most simple forms of logic integrated circuit (as used in computing, digital control systems, etc.). There are several different types of gate (NOT, AND, OR, NAND, NOR, XOR, and XNOR).

Germanium

The substance from which the original transistors were made. These days most semiconductor components are based on silicon, but germanium is still used to some extent (mainly for diodes). Devices based on germanium are more vulnerable to heat damage than are silicon based components.

Hard clipping

See 'clipping'.

Hertz

See 'Frequency'.

Highpass

See filtering

Integrated circuit (i.c.)

A semiconductor component which can provide the equivalent of anything from two to over a million components. Integrated circuits are much used in modern circuits as they permit quite complex circuits to be built at low cost.

Jack

A type of audio connector, much used for headphones and electronic music systems. Most instruments are fitted with standard (6.35mm/0.25') jack sockets, as are many of the projects in this book. There are also smaller (2.5mm and 3.5mm) types, and stereo versions, so you need to be careful to order the right type.

Kilohertz

See 'Frequency'.

Kilohm

See 'Ohm'.

Light emitting diode (L.E.D.)
A diode that produces light if it is fed with an electric current. Unlike an ordinary filament bulb, this is a polarised component which must be connected around the right way or it will not produce any light.

Linear (lin)
See 'Logarithmic'

Logarithmic (log)
In an electronic project context this describes a type of potentiometer. It is one which has a form of non-linear control characteristic (e.g. it does not provide half maximum resistance when adjusted to a middle setting). This type of potentiometer is used in volume controls and similar applications, but linear potentiometers are used in virtually all other applications.

Lowpass
See filtering

Megohm
See 'Ohm'.

Merge unit
A MIDI merge unit takes two or more MIDI signals and combines then to produce a single output signal. This is actually quite difficult to achieve properly. Simple methods of mixing the signals result in them being scrambled together to produce a meaningless output signal. Practical merge units are complex devices which are based on microprocessors.

Metal film
A type of resistor, and a very high quality type.

MIDI
I have seen various explanations for this acronym. It officially stands for 'musical instruments digital interface'. It is a form of computer style interface which enables one musical instrument to control another. These days the controlling device is often a computer or a dedicated sequencer rather than a musical instrument. The hardware and software (the method of coding note on/off information, etc.) are both rigidly standardised, so any MIDI unit should work properly with any other MIDI equipped devices.

MIDI choke

A term used to describe what happens if a system is called upon to transmit more data than MIDI can handle. Exactly what happens when MIDI choke occurs depends on the system, but at the very least it is likely that the timing of note on/off messages will be severely disrupted. In an extreme case I suppose it is possible that the MIDI controller would crash, and the system would be brought to a halt.

Mixer

A mixer is a piece of audio equipment which combines two or more audio sources to produce a single audio output. For example, a mixer is used to combine the outputs from the instruments in a MIDI system. The combined output signal is then fed to an amplifier, recorder, or whatever. Mixers are also used within some pieces of electronic equipment, including several types of effects unit.

Mono

In a MIDI context 'mono' means that only one note per channel is possible. In MIDI mode 2 an instrument is truly monophonic as operation on only one channel is possible, but in mode 4 (formerly known as mono mode) it is possible for an instrument to operate monophonically on several channels. The instrument is then polyphonic, while it is the MIDI channels that are monophonic. The term 'mono' is perhaps a bit misleading in this respect.

MOS

An acronym for 'metal oxide silicon', and a form of technology used for producing some transistors and integrated circuits. Most MOS devices are sensitive to static electricity, and must be kept away from or protected from even modest static charges.

Multi-core

The type of solder used for electrical and electronic work (which includes electronic project building). The multiple cores in question are cores of flux.

Nanofarad

See 'Farad'.

Nibble

A group of four bits (half a byte!).

Notch filter

A filter that enables most signals to pass through to the output. However, signals over a small range of frequencies are greatly reduced, and may even be totally removed. Notch filtering is used to produce the phasing effect.

Ohm

The main unit of electrical resistance. One ohm is quite a small amount of resistance, and so resistances are often expressed in kilohms or megohms. One kilohm is one thousand ohms, and a megohm is one million ohms (one thousand kilohms).

Omni

When 'omni' is 'on', an instrument will respond to messages on any MIDI channel. When 'omni' is 'off', the instrument will only respond to one particular channel (modes 2 and 3), or each voice will be assigned to a particular channel (mode 4).

Operational amplifier (op amp)

A general purpose amplifier that was originally designed for use in analogue computers (to perform mathematical operations). These days an operational amplifier is normally a small integrated circuit which is much used in audio and electronic music applications.

Opto-isolator

This is an electronic component which consists of a light emitting diode (LED) and a photocell of some kind. The light output of the LED is directed at the photocell, and the two components are housed in an opaque plastic case. The point of an opto-isolator is that it enables a switching action to be coupled from the LED at the input to the photo cell at the output, even though there is no direct electrical connection between them. The light provides the coupling. Opto-isolators are used at all MIDI inputs, where the electrical isolation helps to minimise problems with earth loops, stray coupling of digital noise into audio circuits, etc.

Oscillator

This is simply a circuit that generates a series of electrical pulses. Oscillators are much used in practically all types of electronic circuit.

Patch-bay

A MIDI patch-bay is a device which is used to provide the desired interconnections between the units in a MIDI system. The 'IN's and 'OUT's of every MIDI unit are connected to sockets on the patch-bay unit. Controls on the patch-bay are then used to connect everything together in the desired manner. The main point of using a patch-bay is that it enables the system to be reconfigured very quickly and easily. The more up-market units can be switched from one configuration to another under MIDI control. These more complex units usually feature some 'extras' such as MIDI merging and filtering.

Phase shift

This is where a signal is effectively delayed by a certain number of cycles, or a certain part of a cycle. Phase shifts are normally expressed in degrees, and there are 360 degrees per cycle. Thus a signal that is shifted by 180 degrees is delayed by half a cycle, and one which is shifted by 720 degrees is delayed by two cycles. Note that a phase shift and a true delay (as provided by a delay line) are not the same. The delay time provided by a phase shift circuit is frequency dependent. The higher the input frequency, the shorter the delay represented by 'X' number of cycles. A delay line provides a delay time that is independent of the input frequency.

Picofarad

See 'Farad'.

Pin

This can either be a terminal of an integrated circuit (or other components with pin-like terminals), or a solder pin. Solder pins are connected to a circuit board, and then the connections from the board to off-board components are made via these pins. Solder pins are more convenient than direct connections to the board, and provide much more reliable results. One millimetre diameter pins are needed for the 0.1 inch stripboard used for the projects in this book.

Polarised

Normally used to describe a two lead component that must be fitted round the right way if it is to function properly (e.g. electrolytic capacitor). It is also used to describe plugs and sockets that have some sort of mechanical 'key' so that they can only be connected one way round.

Port

A port is merely some form of electrical connector on a computer (or other piece of electronics) to enable it to be connected to some peripheral device. MIDI 'IN', 'OUT', and 'THRU' sockets are all examples of ports. The alternative term 'interface' is sometimes used.

Potentiometer

A variable resistor which has three terminals. Two terminals connect to opposite ends of the track which provides the resistance. There is a fixed resistance between these two terminals. The third connects to the 'wiper', and there is a variable amount of resistance between this and the other two terminals. This is the type of component used in volume controls, tone controls, etc.

Preset resistor

This is a form of potentiometer, or variable resistor. It is designed to fit onto a circuit board rather on a front panel. Preset resistors normally have to be adjusted using a small screwdriver, although some have a small built-in control knob.

Printed crcuit board (PCB)

A printed circuit is a board on which electronic circuits are constructed. Stripboard is a form of proprietary printed circuit which can accommodate practically any circuit. Normal printed circuit boards are designed to take one particular circuit, and are unusable with any other circuits

Printed circuit (PC) mounting

A term which is used to describe components that have both leadout wires coming from the same end, and which are intended for vertical mounting on a printed circuit board. It is most often applied to capacitors, and these are also known as radial capacitors. Any component which is designed for direct mounting on a printed circuit board can be described as a PC type.

Program change

Most instruments and other items of MIDI equipment make use of 'programs'. In an instrument for example, these are a series of preset control settings that give a range of different sounds. Program change messages therefore permit the required sounds to be selected at the appropriate times. Note that other items of MIDI equipment such as mixers and effects units are often controlled via program change messages.

Radial

See 'Printed circuit (PC) mounting'.

Rectifier

Much the same as a diode, but designed to handle much higher power levels.

Resistor
Common electronic component having two leadout wires. It can be connected either way round. The value is normally marked using a four band colour code .

Ribbon cable
Simply a ribbon-like multi-way electrical cable. The 'rainbow' ribbon cable that has a different coloured insulation for each wire is very good for wiring-up electronic projects.

Semiconductor
Components such as diodes, transistors, and integrated circuits which are made from a semiconductor material such as germanium or silicon.

Serial
MIDI is a form of serial communications system, which simply means that is sends information one 'bit' at a time. Parallel systems send data several 'bits' at a time, and are usually much faster. They need multi-way connecting cables though, and often have very restricted ranges (a couple of metres in some cases). Although slower, a serial system is more practical for many applications.

Silicon
The substance from which most modern semiconductor components (transistors, diodes, integrated circuits, etc.) are constructed. Other substances are also used, such as germanium, but are relatively rare.

Soft clipping
See 'Clipping'.

Solder pin
See 'Pin'.

Source
The name given to one of the terminals of a field effect transistor (f.e.t.).

Stand-off
These are usually in the form of small plastic clips which are used to mount a circuit board inside a case, and hold the board a few millimetres clear of the case. Some types are fixed to the board and (or) the case via self-tapping screws, and these provide what is usually a much more reliable method of mounting.

Stray pickup

The wiring in an electronic project can act a bit like an aerial, and will pick up radio signals, 'hum' from mains wiring, etc. In an audio frequency project, which includes musical effects units, this can result in unwanted 'buzzes' and other sounds on the output signal. Ideally, projects which have wiring that is vulnerable to this problem should be fitted in a metal case earthed to the circuit's negative supply rail. However, if all the wiring is kept very short there will usually be no significant pick-up if a non-metallic case is used. Audio leads should be good quality screened types in order to prevent them from picking up electrical noise.

Stripboard

A thin board made from an insulating material and drilled all over with 1mm diameter holes on a 0.1 inch (2.54mm) matrix. Copper strips run along the rows of holes on one side of the board. All but one of the projects in this book are based on a piece of stripboard.

System messages

These are the MIDI messages that do not carry a channel number in the header byte. They are therefore responded to by every piece of equipment in the system that recognises them. These are mainly the MIDI clock and associated messages.

THRU

A 'THRU' socket is to be found on many items of MIDI equipment. It simply provides a replica of what is received on the 'IN' socket. In a multi-unit system the 'THRU' socket on one unit can be coupled through to the 'IN' socket of the next unit ('chain' connection).

THRU box

Not all MIDI units have THRU sockets, and in particular, they are often absent from keyboard instruments. A THRU box has a MIDI 'IN' socket and several 'THRU' output sockets. In a multi-unit system the OUT socket of the controller connects to the 'IN' socket of the THRU box. The 'THRU' outputs then connect to the 'IN' sockets of each instrument etc. in the system ('star' connection).

Tinning

Tinning simply means covering something with a thin layer of solder. The end of a soldering iron's bit should be kept well tinned so that it makes good thermal contact with the joints. It is also a good idea to tin the ends of leads and tags prior to soldering them together.

Toggle switch

A switch that is operated via a small lever (called a 'dolly').

Transistor

A three terminal electronic component which can provide amplification. The terminals are called the base, collector and emitter.

UART

This is an acronym which stands for 'universal asynchronous receiver/transmitter'. It is a type of digital integrated circuit which is used to convert parallel data into serial data (transmitter), and to convert serial data into parallel data (receiver). In an electronic music context UARTs have become important because they are used to provide much of the signal processing at MIDI inputs and outputs.

Variable resistor

See 'Potentiometer'.

Veroboard

A proprietary name for the stripboard which is used as the basis of all but one of the projects in this book.

VMOS

A type of field effect transistor.

XLR

This is a heavy-duty form of three way audio connector which is used a great deal in professional audio equipment. In particular, it is used for balanced line inputs on professional mixing and recording equipment. XLR connectors are also used to carry MIDI interconnections, although in practice they are little used for this purpose. 5 way type A DIN connectors are the other type of connector sanctioned by the MIDI specification, and are far more popular.

Index